A ROSIE LIFE IN ITALY 2

WHAT HAVE WE DONE?

ROSIE MELEADY

ENVY PUBLISHING

Copyright © 2021 by Rosie Meleady

ISBN: 9798752849640

All rights reserved.

No part of this book may be reproduced in any form or by any electronic or mechanical means, including information storage and retrieval systems, without written permission from the author, except for the use of brief quotations in a book review. V3

BEFORE YOU START…

See more from Rosie and join her newsletter on: www.rosiemeleady.com

Social Media: @ARosieLifeInItaly

On Rosie's blog and newsletter you'll find she likes to talk about buying a house in Italy, renovating, travel in Italy, restoring furniture, books about Italy, life and pets in Italy

While this book is based on fact, the author has used poetic licence, has exaggerated and created some fictional scenes and people. Some names of real characters and places have also been changed for protection… of the author.

To Ronan,

You would be shocked at the amount of stuff I write about you. Thanks for not reading my books.

Love,

Your Darling Wife.

1

HOUSE TO RENT IN ITALY: €600

Ronan is brave. He is going into the spooky attic with just the light on his phone. I stand at the door, egging him on through the sheets of grey cobwebs. He gives me an audio guided tour of his encounters.

"That's a bath, but nothing special, just one of those half baths. And there's an old spring base for a bed and an old chair."

We had stood at the attic doorway many times before on our brief pre-owner visits, staring at the outlines in the darkness, back-lit by the light dodging its way in between the shifted roof tiles above. It was like we were in an episode of Storage Wars. "That's a cast iron bath right there. That looks like an old bed... I wonder what is in those boxes?" Ronan would sometimes chip in "That's one hundred dollars right there," in his best Storage Wars American accent.

Two hours before, on that already hot morning in May 2020, we had signed on the dotted line... well actually our Italian friend Lucia, who we had given power of attorney to, had signed on the dotted line to proclaim ownership of the house on our behalf.

In so doing, the argumentative eight cousins and their old 'Uncle' Busy-Body Francesca were released from their generational ties to the hundred-year-old, three-storey, 22-roomed derelict villa and its interior doors they tried to rob a few weeks before.

We were now the owners of the lot and free to rummage amongst the junk left behind to find potential hidden treasure or enough rubbish to fill a dump.

I had been dying to explore the attic, or I should say, I had been dying to send Ronan in to explore the attic. I had been afraid to venture in there in case we found something valuable and felt compelled to tell the people we were buying from about it.

It's a walk-in attic from the landing on the second floor. The ancient wooden door is complete with a broken latch held from creaking open by a piece of leftover electrical wire. The other side of the landing of the central stairs leads to what was apartment number four, comprising four rooms – one large, two medium, one small and a small bathroom, all connected by a short hallway. There are two near-identical apartments on the ground floor and first floor.

Opening the attic door also unleashes a blast of hot dusty air which the undisturbed space has been holding in its tiled lung for decades. This room's use has yet to be decided, but I have a feeling it will be one of the most beautiful rooms in the entire house. Perhaps a cinema room or yoga room for

A Rosie Life In Italy 2

groups some day. Ronan's guided audio tour of the inner sanctum immediately confirms some of our guesses of the shadowy outlines in the attic room.

He goes deeper. "There are some bottles... they're empty. Old whiskey bottles and grappa."

"This looks like a gramophone stand or an old radio... there's a bird nest in it..." Ronan's tall, broad-shouldered frame is blocking the light from my torch reaching the outlined object.

I can hear his hand rummaging in straw.

"A bird's nest?" I'm thinking out loud. "But there's no light, no entry from the roof... RONAN that's not a bird's nest, that's a rat's nest, get your hand out of there!"

Not just his hand, but his whole six foot self launches out of attic and back onto the landing. We both stand still at the door, listening for squeaks or movement.

"Were there any babies?" I ask feebly after a moment, trying not to be horrified.

"No, I don't think so..."

"It's probably an old one," I say reassuringly, as there is no sound of movement, just the rustle of the leaves outside.

"Yep, probably, there are no rat droppings around either," he says, but I know he's not so sure.

"So go back in and get it," I urge him.

"What?"

"The gramophone. I want to see it, go get it man."

"You go!"

"I can't." I try to think of an excuse. "I have a frozen shoulder."

"Your shoulder has been grand for months!"

I had two frozen shoulders for over a year. I went to a young osteopath doctor in Italy a few months after the first one seized up. My Italian friend and local agriturismo owner, Lucia, had told me about this private clinic. "They are the best". Everything is always the best to her until something better comes along. As it was a private clinic, I could make an appointment without being resident. The young doctor took the opportunity to try out his English on me. I'm sure he was trying to say that I was pretty young to have such a severe problem, but instead he told me I was pretty and young to have such a severe frozen shoulder. I was laughing to myself until he stuck a needle deep into my shoulder in three different spots and pumped it with cortisone.

He then sent me into the physiotherapist next door. This guy was young and cheerful and determined to help me learn Italian during every visit. He had done seven years in college and had his own practice. Chatting casually during the second or third visit, I find out his mam is the same age as me. Okay, she had him as a teenager, but still I left feeling old. Probably too old to be taking on a major renovation.

My shoulders are definitely not healed enough for me to wander into the spooky attic. To be fair, they will never be that healed because there is no way I was going to be brave enough to go into that attic.

A Rosie Life In Italy 2

But Ronan is brave. He puts on his work gloves and goes boldly where no man has gone in over ten years. He heaves the dusty, wood-veneered unit out, complete with rat's nest.

I poke it with a stick. It crumbles in straw clumps onto the floor. It has been empty for a long time.

It's an international radio from around the 1920s, probably the hub of knowledge and entertainment in the house. I can imagine the family gathering around it during the war, listening for updates and dancing around it when the war was over.

I feel another restoration project coming on. It will definitely have a place of pride in the house, as long as Ronan the Brave gets rid of the rat's nest first.

Next, he pulls out an old iron washstand with a marble top and mirror intact. A high pitch sound comes up my esophagus. Ronan releases the washstand in the doorway and jumps back. "What's wrong?"

"Nothing!"

"Did you see a rat?"

"No."

"What was that sound you made?"

"I don't know. I think it was... delight?"

"I've never heard you make that sound in all the years we've been together," he says, bewildered. "Have you not ever been delighted before now?"

"I've never experienced it either, but I've always wanted a washstand, since watching John Wayne Westerns with my parents. Or maybe it was Little House on the Prairie? Washstands and writing bureaus, you know what I'm like."

Ronan's standing there with cobwebs hanging from him like seaweed hanging from an old lobster dragged from the deep, looking at me like I'm a terrible smell. I think it's confusion. "After 25 years together, I'm still learning about you," he says before stepping back into the darkness. With a few more tugs and me shouting at him to mind the walls, mind the door, don't hurt yourself and to hurry. The washstand is finally out beside the gramophone on the small landing.

"Mam, can I borrow some of these books?" Luca calls out from a room in the next apartment.

"Borrow? Take what you like honey this is all ours now," I say like a lady of a manor as I lean on the banister that wobbles under my hand. A piece of loose plaster from the railing base bounces down the stairwell to its final crash spot on the ground floor. I find our 17-year-old son looking through the bookshelves in what was a bedroom.

"This guy had a really cool signature look." Luca holds out the opened hardback cover of Dante's Inferno, a part of every Italian household. In beautiful pen and ink calligraphy, the name Paolo Legume is inscribed on the page. The signature is very similar to the one of Miss Piggy's I used to copy from the Muppet Annual and still use when a full signature is required.

"Whoever he was, he seemed to be interested in everything. Look at this." Luca pulls out a full-to-the-brim man drawer. "There's some interesting shit in here, can I have a root in it?"

"Luca, you've just got yourself the job of sorting out the good stuff from the rubbish. But don't start now, start tomorrow. It's getting dark and we need to head back home to the dogs."

"Look at the books, Mam," Luca points to a pile of books on the bed frame. There's an Italian version of the Bagvah Gita, a bible, along with a free book from the Jehovah Witnesses. "Wouldn't exploring religions be unusual in the 1940s or 50s? He must have been really curious about other people's beliefs or an open-minded man. And he was also big into learning languages. I've found a Spanish-Italian dictionary, a German-Italian dictionary and an English lesson book from the 1940s."

Luca has me curious now. "You've just got a job promotion, you can work on figuring out who Mr Bean was, he might give us clues to the history of the house... Take that English lesson book home, it might help me learn Italian."

"I'm not sure if it will help, Mam. I've spent at least an hour laughing through the lessons of how to talk like an Englishman."

"Give me a look."

Twenty minutes later Ronan finds us reading through the 'How to speak like an English man' lessons, with laughter-tears rolling down our faces.

"What's so funny?"

"We'll tell you in the car. Let's go before it gets completely dark."

To me, these books and the stuff found in the attic are better than gold. All I need now is for Ronan to find an old rocking horse, doll house and a pirate treasure box and all my childhood fantasies about renovating an old house in a foreign land will have come true.

We had renovated houses twice before in Ireland. Neither ended well. We had said never again, but this one felt different. It doesn't need as much done. The house is dry and in good condition considering it has not been lived in for so long. There's no sign of damp on the thick walls other than the front corner room, where the water has hit for years after pouring in from the street over the blocked gully.

We had been in the house once before when there was a downpour and had watched the bubbling water rushing down the street passing every other gateway on the street, which had cleverly built up their driveway to be by-passed the river, until it got to ours and flowed rapidly over the blocked grill. "This is Umbria, not Venice, right?" I had said to Ronan as we watched the river rapids on the road form a canal along the front of the house, flow down the side path and create a huge pool in the dip between the house and the shed.

"It's not Venice, but I think we have found where to park the gondola."

In the car, on the way home to the house we have been renting for nearly three years, I remember the English-Italian lesson book Luca has. "So give us an Italian lesson from the 'learn English' book, Luca," I say seriously, knowing what's ahead.

"Well in this chapter," he starts, "we learn all the important phrases to tell someone we have been in prison, as we learn that Claude has been in prison, but not for killing his mother-in-law as the previous lesson would have led us to believe."

"Hullo Claude: Ciao Claude."

"Hullo Ethel: Ciao Ethel."

"Where have you been lately?: Dove sei stato ultimamente."

"I have been to prison: Sono stato in prison."

"What for?: Cosa per? Or Per che cosa?"

The police said I took a pekingese from a car: La polizia disse che avevo preso un pechinese da una macchina."

Luca continues the translation of the dialogue lesson:

"And did you?"

"No, I borrowed it!"

"Why did you borrow it?"

"I wanted to give it some exercise."

"I wanted to take it off its lead and take it up the road!"

"And take it to show my aunt. So I took it out of the car and put it down on the pavement."

"But a policeman came across the street and took me away to prison."

"Let's go," he said.

"Let me think," I said.

"You can think in prison," he said.

"Let's be reasonable," I said.

"Shut up," he said.

So I said to the judge: "Be kind" and the judge said to me: "let's look at your record."

"Nine times in prison, disgraceful!"

"I don't like odd numbers."

"Let's make it even, let's make it ten."

"What the hell?" Ronan is looking as confused as I was when reading the earlier lessons.

"They were all very important phrases for Italians to know when starting out learning English in the 1940s," laughs Luca.

That night I lie in bed thinking about the house as usual, but particularly the Venetian canal problem. We could solve it by building up the driveways. I felt better after spending the day in the house treasure hunting. It wasn't too bad. The windows were intact, and doors secure. Other than the one hole that needed repairing, the roof looked good. The house looked like we could live it in sooner rather than later. It wouldn't be a perfectly finished house, but it would be a beautiful home.

How wrong I was.

2

GIRL'S WORLD: £26

"But there's just a head? She doesn't even have a body."

"Her eyes change colour if you turn her upside down and back again. This one is even better than the one my cousins have," I said. My 11-year-old self looked in awe at the head in the box, stacked with the other hundred heads.

My mother looked aghast. "Are you really sure that's what you want? A Girl's World?"

"A Girl's World with changing eye colours and hair dyes."

I saw the price on a big sign beside it; £26. I was so glad Santa made these things, as my family could never afford it.

With an older sister and three older brothers who had lots of friends, I grew up in a party house. I thought having three different parties going on every weekend was a normal household occurrence. There would be one in the attic room, which my dad converted with oddments of wood as a room for Jimmy. Weekend sessions there usually involved two guitars and his friend Gary singing Elvis and Willie Nelson.

The parties in the lifeguard's hut in the back garden usually involved Pink Floyd and Jethro Tull and my brother Peter playing the saxophone or the piano, which was gradually sinking into the ground because of the sagging, rotting floorboards. The hut was Peter's room since he left home to live in the garden at 14, after he decided he had outgrown the family's small bungalow.

The other simultaneous weekend parties happened in the back room and were punk-themed, along with The Clash and someone singing The Boomtown Rats... usually Gary. Gary got around as he was a friend of two brothers with two separate friend groups, so he drifted between parties up and down the homemade wooden stairs that my bed was tucked under. I eventually moved out of my grandmother's room and got my own 'space' – a bed under the homemade wooden staircase which creaked and croaked like it could collapse at any moment. The Meleady's house was the party house, where everyone went to get drunk and have a good time on weekends and Christmas Eve.

Little did I know that my Christmas-loving, magic-creating mother, was going to get me, the youngest of her five kids, whatever gift I wanted no matter if it did cost a week's grocery shopping, to make sure the last year of Santa visiting our house was fantastic.

Santa, as usual, arrived at about 11pm on Christmas eve, and there she was in all her glory, my very own Girl's World mannequin head – a blank canvas for my makeup and hair creations. She was too precious to take out of the box, I wanted to wait until I had a full day to marvel at each individual item and follow the guide to creating my masterpiece 'looks'. I went back to bed and fell asleep happily.

I came out to the sitting room on Christmas morning and there she still was, my Girl's World head suction cupped to the table where I had left her to do my first creative masterpiece, turning her into a princess... but 'they' had got to her before me.

Some bastardly, brother-friend-group had used the sacred dye pens to streak her hair every shade, given her punk makeup, black eyeliner and to cap it all off, had drawn a swastika in the centre of her forehead.

I could never look at her the same again. To this day, none of them will admit who did it.

Other than that, Christmas always seemed such a magical and special time, especially as my granny, who lived with us, usually survived another round of last rites just a couple of weeks before Christmas. Seven years in a row she sank into a sort of coma in her bed, triggered by a self-diagnosed bout of bronchitis or pneumonia.

Everyone would gather to say their farewells. The Last Rites Biscuit Tin would be taken out of Nanny's wardrobe. Inside it lay a small, white lace tablecloth, a crucifix with its own stand held together with yellowing sticky tape that had long since lost its stick, a taper candle that was also held together in the middle with the same yellowing tape and a small bottle of Lourdes holy water that had been there so long brown bits of matter were floating around in it. She was ready for anything.

The candle was never lit, not only because no one could ever find matches to light it with when the crucial moment arose, but my mam had a huge fear of lit candles in the house; a lit candle would surely be forgotten about, a curtain would catch light no matter how far away it was, the whole stone house would go up like a tinderbox and we'd all burn to a crisp.

The priest was called. He'd arrive and say his bit, give Nanny and her bad chest the last rites and by some miracle her eyes would flicker open and she'd be all surprised to see everyone there. A cup of tea would be suggested, but a glass of whiskey accepted as it cut through whatever had her bad chest critical for the last few hours or days. And sure, while everyone's here, why don't you all have a drink? Inevitably, a celebration party would ensue. We called these Nanny's wake parties.

One of the enormous benefits, in my eyes, to having kids, was that I could have magical Christmases again, except this time I was the magician. My brother Tony would come to stay and together we'd set the stage. Balloons pressed into the fireplace ashes would be Santa's butt print. Wellies with painted on mud on the soles were strategically walked from the fireplace to the stockings and Tony's signature masterpiece was him going off into the back field at midnight to find a fresh cowpat, carry it back on a shovel and put it on top of his car. It was usually discovered by my kids, Izzy and Luca, just before lunch on Christmas day, "Bloody Rudolf shit on my car again," Tony would grumble. Of course Santa was real, who on earth would put poo on their car?

Santa for Izzy was easy. She always chose whatever was pumped at them through TV ads. Luca was difficult.

A Rosie Life In Italy 2

I still find it fascinating that you can make kids from the same recipe and come up with such different results. Izzy is social and high energy. Luca is so laid back he's nearly lying down. He was the easiest child ever to bring up. Never an ounce of trouble and careful about himself and others. He still has never been to a doctor because he never got more than a cold and has never seen the inside of a hospital. Touch wood or touch iron, as is the case in Italy.

Luca knows what he wants and what he doesn't want. I imagined if I had a boy he would be into every sport like his grandfather and father, adventurous and with all the classes I would send him to, he would be a black belt, musician and able to speak three languages before he was twelve.

But Luca had other ideas. "No thank you," was his catchphrase that we still know him for. He'd bargain with me over what point he could give up the new hobby I had signed him up for.

"Okay, if you still don't like it when you get your yellow belt then you can give up," I'd say.

I thought he'd love Tai Kwon Do enough by then that he'd stick with it. A year of twice weekly classes, leaving was never mentioned again, but as the examiner handed him his yellow belt with congratulations, my eight-year-old looked up at me with his big blue puddle eyes. "Okay, so I'm done now. I don't have to come back, right?"

How could I argue?

Every year, all he ever asked Santa for was paper and a pencil. "I just like to draw, that's all I want."

This might sound sweet and easy, but for a Christmas freak like me, giving my kid a ream of paper and a pencil was not an option. "Come on Luca, think of something different."

It is the worst thing I could have said to the child with the wicked sense of humour.

"Okay, I want a six-foot llama and a pig on a pickup truck," he said without a second thought.

It's amazing what you can find online. A blow-up lama took pride of place beside the tree and matchbox-size pickup truck had a farmyard toy pig taped in the back sat in the tree. I love a Christmas challenge.

Even though my kids are now 24 and 17, I still crave idyllic Christmases. However, Christmas since moving to Italy three years ago was a bigger challenge than the six-foot llama. I felt we hadn't had a proper family Christmas here yet. This was mostly down to us not finding the familiar foods that made Christmas, Christmas; a rental house with a dodgy oven that would switch off whenever it chose and refuse to come on again until such time it chose; a small sitting room where every corner had at least one door, so no room for a Christmas tree.

And the garish tiles on the floors, walls and fireplace didn't quite give the ideal background to my much-loved Christmas decorations collection. But this year was going to be different. This year we had our own house, and we were going to have the perfect Pinterest Christmas no matter what.

We had just finished the purchase of a 22-roomed derelict villa in Umbria in May, which I nicknamed the Sighing

House, and whatever it took, I was going to have Christmas with my family there.

The day we agreed to buy The Sighing House, the first thing I had spotted when I walked in the door was the perfect spot for a massive Christmas tree. As I walked around that day I saw beyond the cobwebs and peeling paint and imagined a turkey in the oven of a beautiful fitted kitchen with black marble tops, a stove burning orange in the huge fireplace, lit candles (unless my mother made it over), twinkling lights on a garland over the fire mantel, our two dogs and two cats slumbering together on a fireside rug. Stockings hanging on the fireplace, garlands festooning the hallway banisters, strings of lights hanging from the three balconies. Cinnamon apples, Christmas dinner cooking and pine lingering in the air.

I imagined the excitement bubbling up when Izzy would arrive home from London through the front door to the warm hall and seeing the tree with the gifts piled under it including the mandatory ream of paper and pencil I still buy as a tradition every year for Luca.

The joy, the laughter, the baking, the board games, the annual jigsaw being done, the trash TV shows, the Christmas movies, the thick Italian hot chocolate, the coziness of home and family.

Moving in to our new home by Christmas was going to happen, not just because my idyllic Christmas needed to come back to life, but because we had no other choice.

I planned weddings and Ronan photographed them. Our business hadn't had a wedding for 12 months because of the

COVID-19 pandemic. By 23rd of December our rent fund pot would run dry and there was no chance of it being topped up until the following year when weddings kicked off again.

No one had expected the pandemic to last to Christmas but here we were with a year of income missed and we needed to tighten our belts and be careful with the funds we had saved to renovate the house, as we were now also living off them.

Like so many, we expected the flip of the calendar from 2020 to 21 would wipe the slate clean and we would be back to normal. I knew this expectation was just a hope and out of our control, but whatever happened, we were going to have the perfect Christmas in our newly renovated, previously derelict house. That was something within my control, wasn't it?

3

22-ROOMED DERELICT HOUSE: €120K

"Holy crap Rosie, there's that high-pitched noise again!" We're in the car reversing out of the gate and Ronan has jammed on the brakes, thinking he's hit a cat or something. "You're going to cause an accident. What the hell are you delighted about now?"

"She's coming back!" I squeal. It's the only way to describe the sound I make.

"When?"

"Twenty-three days, five hours and 12 minutes." My eyes are filling up so much that I'm finding it hard to read the rest of her text through the blur, but I can still make out Ronan's Adam's apple rising and falling with a gulp. He pulls me close across the divide and kisses my head.

After 70 days, the pandemic lockdown in Italy had recently ended, while other countries were still in the throes of lockdowns and increasing numbers. Our 23-year-old daughter Izzy had moved to London for a job only two months before

COVID hit Italy. It soon became rife in London, suspending her job and restricting people's movements.

The nature of her work in the world of TV meant those she worked with dispersed back to their home countries. The friendships she was forming were still fragile, not intimate enough to call on when you are desperately alone during a worldwide pandemic. Izzy, not being a resident in Italy, could not come home to us. Instead, she had struggled through quarantine lockdowns alone in London for three months.

We watched social media posts of people enjoying being forced to spend time with their families as the world came to a standstill.

"Off for another hike... family card night... Friday night is dress up and pretend we are going out night," they chirped. Family bubbles making the most of the time while ours was splashed across Italy, London and Ireland, separated by closed borders and with no idea when it would be safe for us to see each other again.

She had dealt well with ten weeks in solitary isolation in a flat in London, but my Mamma Bear protection instincts had been kicking in big time when the cracks of desperation hit both of us. I thanked the gods for video chat. I tried to perk her up when I could see her dip, but there were times we both slid down and just had a cry together.

Loneliness, boredom and fear all played their part. Video chat didn't replace a long hug, physical touch, making each other a cup of tea, holding hands while we talked over fluffy shows on the TV. Watching things we would never make on cookery shows and Great British Bake Off. Reruns of sitcoms.

The odd Disney movie that induced memories of Christmas feelings, of coziness, hot chocolate and cuddles under blankets on the sofa.

For months, Italy wasn't letting non-residents in. We waited, hoping the ban would lift. We waited three months. Three months of not knowing when it would end. She sat in her one-roomed, rented apartment alone. Each day, we spent hours on video apps. Just to feel we were together, we would sometimes just leave it on and go about what we were doing; cooking, reading, writing, going to sleep. Both of us knew the other would sometimes cry when the call would end. We grew to understand that being sad was okay. This situation was not normal, but it was our new normal. Nothing is more heartbreaking than knowing your kid needs you, but there is no way you can get to them.

But now she had booked a flight for the first day borders were opening for international travel. She was coming home. To a new home in a new country.

Buying a house in Italy was a 'someday' dream ever since I came on a writer's retreat to Tuscany and brought my little family with me 14 years previously. It was the first time any of us had been to Italy and the first time our then 4-year-old and 10-year-old kidlets saw real fairies, their little lanterns sparking across the poppy fields beside the yellow stone villa we were staying at, surrounded by hills of olive groves and upside-down ice cream cone trees. Fresh pizza and pasta, olives and gelato flavours we had never imagined.

Ronan nearly spoiled the illusion by catching one said fairy in his hand to show the kids a firefly's flashing bum up close, but I grabbed his hand shut before he opened it. That firefly's life was sacrificed in the name of keeping magic alive.

As it does with everyone, a lot happened in the 14 years that followed our first trip to Italy.

When our family home was repossessed by a bank in Ireland, we moved to Italy with very little planning, in the space of three weeks. We'd stay positive by listing what each of us wanted from an ideal family home when we could ever afford one again. While mine centred around socialising, Ronan's vision focused on not having to drive me home from socialising. While Luca's focused on being able to escape from us socialising.

Izzy's list of needs ranged from a non-dribble shower to a big enough sofa we can all sit on together like the old days.

One thing we all agree on was that it had to be 'turn key' and not a renovation project. The kids had spent most of their childhood years in renovation projects and Ronan and I had nearly divorced several times over how to tile a bathroom or put flat-pack furniture together.

We went to view The Sighing House on Lake Trasimeno in Italy out of nosiness. It had been derelict for ten years and an extensive renovation project, so it would need to be someone else's dream. We told the estate agent it wasn't for us. The €240k asking price was not in our range, ours was half that.

We stopped off on the way home to buy some fruit and wine and that's when the estate agent called me to say the offer, we didn't realise we had made, was accepted.

It was too good an opportunity to miss. Yes, we committed to buying it, when we weren't even looking for somewhere to buy. Basically, we bought The Sighing House by accident while buying bananas.

We were due to close the sale on 10th of March 2020, which instead became the day Italy went into the strictest lockdown at the time in the Western World. Ordered to stay within our homes, our appointment was cancelled. Instead, I planted sunflower seeds, hoping that by the time they bloom this nightmare called COVID would be over.

The pandemic also meant my destination wedding business I had grown over the last 20 years, went into free fall as, one by one, my wedding planning clients cancelled or postponed, followed by Ronan's wedding photography clients. With all our wedding planning and photography work gone for the year, it was touch and go whether or not we could buy it, but we eventually closed the sale on the 26th of May 2020.

Ronan carried me across the threshold. Due to him having a bad back and me having plenty of extra pounds since he carried me across our first threshold 25 years previously, we did the manoeuvre piggy-back style.

Now that we were the owners, we were viewing the house through fresh eyes.

At that point, I didn't quite know what we were the owners of. I thought it was one house with an extensive garden. But apparently on paper it was still registered as four separate properties and there was a vineyard. It turned out the 'vineyard' was the five remaining vines at the end of the garden, four alive and one dead.

There was no time to waste. We were going to be in this house by Christmas. This was not just a fanciful idea. We were originally supposed to stay in Giovanni's rental for only one year, and we were now in year three. The local Comune was now aware we were there full time, which would get him into trouble with the tax office if they prodded a little. The pandemic's stay in place restrictions had been his excuse to them and he had told them we would be out by Christmas.

It was a small town and everyone knew everyone's business and movements, so there was no getting away with it. Someone had it in for him, it seemed, in the local Comune and was on his case. He didn't like putting us under pressure, but whether the house was finished or not, we needed to be out of his place before Christmas.

However, with no income for the year – a year that should have been our most profitable – and just our house renovation savings to live on, the sooner we were no longer paying €600 for rent each month, the better.

COVID had had a knock-on effect on our finances in more ways than one. We still could not travel back to Ireland because of restrictions and Ronan was running out of his medication. This was subsidised in Ireland, so cost us less than €20 a month, but unsubsidised it would be €200 and we would soon need to fork that out each month if travel restrictions continued. I knew he was not taking his medication correctly, resorting to every second day rather than daily like he should, to make it last until we could travel back and save us from forking out €200 each month.

On top of all this, Luca was starting college in October. He had found the perfect four-year digital art course in Florence.

To apply, he needed a portfolio, so he whipped out the five shoe boxes of drawings he had kept carefully, one for each year since he was ten. I had suggested we store these in an attic back in Ireland, but he insisted the shoeboxes were part of our critical supply of things that had to be squashed into the van when we first moved over. With the memories of his fantastical monster creations of his child's mind triggered by his collection, he developed more sophisticated creatures and sketches and was accepted to the course. As we are not residents yet, the full fee of €4,000 needed to be paid upfront for the year. Another chunk out of the pot.

We gave the builders the cutoff date of November 1st; the date we arrived in Italy three years previously. We were giving ourselves wiggle room. Christmas was our absolute limit. After that, money would be tight until payments started coming through for wedding bookings again the following spring.

Our saving grace was that Anto, the builder, was Giovanni's son, so he knew his father's dilemma. However, rather than reassuring me the house would be ready, his solution was to give us regular notifications of other places in the area that we could rent.

"No, we will not be renting again, as we will be moving into the house," I repeated each time he texted a suggestion. I could practically feel him sweating at my 'optimism'. But to me it was not optimism, it was determination driven by desperation, if our money ran out we would have no other choice but to lock up the house and move back to live with my parents in Ireland in their two-bedroomed cottage.

So my determination, disguised as optimism, stayed. It was late May; we had lots of time and the weather was just perfect for the first job we needed to do in the house; clear the compacted mud from the drain that runs under the front gate. The house is on a slight downward slope from the road so for the last ten years at least, rainwater, mud and silt debris has been flowing from the road across the compacted drain to the front of the house and probably been one of the major causes of damp to the north-facing facade.

Ronan unscrews the lock of the front gate and opens it for the first time in years. The compacted mud and leaves are half a foot deep.

We arrived at three o'clock. Five wheelbarrows full later, we have the entrance way cleared within an hour. This feels easy.

Luca and I start work on clearing about 20 years of fallen magnolia leaves and dirt from the front garden and discover an ornate stone border buried around the neglected flower beds. However, there is a section missing. After some searching, we find it was down a covered up mini-sinkhole in the front garden. The hole is about four feet deep. Crouched down, Luca stares into the hole. "A piece of a large concrete water pipe is missing, causing the clay above to fall in and get washed away over the years."

"Please don't tell me that is a sewerage pipe."

"I don't think it is. I think it's a broken rainwater drain. If you look in the direction it's coming from on the road, you can see it's in a direct line with that grill on the other side of the road. It looks like we have a public rainwater drain running right

A Rosie Life In Italy 2

through our garden, probably to the lake eventually, I think... Interesting garden water feature."

It's added to the list of things to be taken care of.

As we own four apartments on paper and a garage outside, we have to pay property tax on all four units until Mick Kelly – our Italian architect, whose name is actually Michele but to us sounds like a typical Irish builder name Mick Kelly and easier to remember pronunciation that way – makes them into one unit on paper and logs it with the commune.

It's common in Italy for one building to be subdivided into 'apartments' for siblings who then go on and have their own families. Our place was divided between three brothers and a sister. The sister was last to leave the house and, as she has Alzheimer's, she is now in a nursing home facility just up the road.

"I think we've done enough for today. Let's head back and get some dinner," Ronan says, closing up the windows we had left open downstairs. The old-fashioned metal rod closing mechanism is stuck on some, others need gentle coaxing to close again. Gentle is not something in Ronan's vocabulary when it comes to sticky windows. Brute force is his chosen method as his hand smashes through a single pane, shattering the glass. I just stand and watch him as he takes it like a pinch of salt, like that was supposed to happen.

"That was lucky. I didn't slice a vein," he chirps, glancing at his unmarked arm. Within a week, he'll do it again with another window and again have a lucky escape.

I note we need to get double glazing soon. Another expense added to the growing 'to be done asap' list and with 33 windows, it would not be cheap. I had hoped we could do a patch-up temporary job and wait until the following year, but now I know this isn't possible. We need double glazing not just for heat purposes, but it will be less breakable with Ronan now in the house.

4

COCKROACH KILLER SPRAY: €9

In what will be the breakfast room with its French doors opening out onto the future courtyard, I wobble a wall tile. Humidity has caused some of the lower ones to 'belly' and when the doorframes were abruptly pried off the walls by the previous owners in their attempt to steal all the interior doors after we agreed to buy the house, the tiles loosened further.

This was the start of it; the reason we had to leave the windows wide open because of the toxic fumes we had caused, or should I say Ronan caused, three weeks earlier. We didn't own the house at the time, but we were close to closing the purchase and we had snuck in the back door and viewed things a little differently as the soon-to-be owners. We couldn't wait to get started, so we didn't wait. I really thought we were going to die a slow death of toxic poisoning after that last visit.

The tile came away easily. I picked off another. It takes three more tiles with it, which loosens the next few. It's like having a back itch that just keeps moving along ahead of the scratch.

"Oh my God, it's a red brick wall."

Ronan does not realise how excited I am by this, but I am suppressing a tightness in my throat and jaw, which we will later discover manifests itself as one of my newly found delighted shrieks. Within minutes of my initial picking at a single loose tile, I have now armed myself with a garden trowel that easily slides into gaps behind tiles and pulls down long stuck-together tiles in sheets that crash to the floor. "It's perfect."

"What do you intend to do with it, paint it?" Ronan asks.

"NO! Leave it as is. A raw red brick wall is very cool. I think I really like it as it is with the white plaster left jagged at the top. It reminds me of Pompeii!"

"Should we wait until we own the house before you do any more?" It's very unlike him to ask such a logical question.

"They already started it when they removed the door frames. They pulled off that section of tile, that wasn't me," I said, pointing to the couple of tiles in the corner that had spurred me on to create the domino effect.

"And anyway, my tile removing is not as drastic as what you are doing," I said, justifying myself as I watched Ronan unscrewing and pulling the grotty aluminium sink off the wall in the corner of the room. The laminated chipboard base breaks up with little effort. The room has a brick fireplace with a protruding chimney. I've already thought about how we will block up the chimney and create a shelved space inside the fireplace for cookery books.

It has a thick wooden beam as a mantle and there are still a variety of random objects on it; a plaque with a prayer to St Francis of Assisi, four different wooden spoons, a souvenir vase from Sorrento and a mystery white pill-box-size container with a sun-bleached label on it. There are some faded drawings of ants or insects on it, and the red and yellow poison symbol of a skull and crossbones is still just about visible. The how-to-use label is faded and I don't have time to translate it.

I'm the one starting to have second thoughts and collywobbles. "Ronan, what if the sale falls through? Could they charge us for destroying the house?" I said as another sheet of bellied tiles smashed to the ground.

"We're doing them a favour, giving whoever gets it a head start," Ronan continued to reef out the remaining wood that had attached itself with years of grease to the tiles behind. After breaking it up with his foot and dumping it outside the back door he returned to inspect the lead outlet pipe cemented into the wall.

"Oooh, is that a cockroach? And are they its eggs?" His face wrinkled up in disapproval.

I went over to where Ronan was half squatted down and pouring some water to form a small puddle in the corner.

"Are they floating? Bad eggs float, isn't that a fact?" he said, staring at the patch.

"Ronan, that's hen's eggs. Bad hen eggs float, I don't think it applies to just any eggs of creatures humans label as unlikeable."

He moved away so I could inspect the large shiny beetle-like creature with a long antenna sitting on the wall, probably looking at us. I like creatures, but this one looked nasty.

"I don't know, I haven't seen a cockroach in 25 years since I was in the States, but the ones I saw were a lot smaller and less black than that. And I don't know what cockroach eggs look like... I think that is just dirt, not eggs, we can just sweep-"

I glanced to my side where Ronan stood with the mysterious white plastic bottle, with the security lid and the big crossbones in red and yellow on the side. I understood the word poison and warning. It was the same picture to illustrate poison in most countries. But that would never deter Ronan. Before I had time to say the full version of 'WTF', he had screwed off the top lid, and took a deep sniff of the contents. While coughing and spluttering, he poured the crystallised powder all over the black dots. As soon as it touched the water, it sizzled and bubbled.

Before I could say 'WTF' again, I was rushing to the door, away from the pungent, sulphur choking smell of invisible fumes the room was now filling with. Such a strong smell from such a small amount could not be a good thing to inhale.

"Get the hell out," I shouted at Ronan as I reached the back door, my nose and mouth covered with my sleeved arm. But he ran the other way. I waited outside in the garden coughing, heaving, spluttering. I made my way to the car, parked at the side of the house as he came out the front door.

A Rosie Life In Italy 2

"I had to get my wallet I'd left in the hallway." He was dry wrenching, holding onto the side of the car.

"Did you kill it?" I said, gasping.

"What?" He asked, rubbing his eyes.

"The cockroach."

"Ah no, it was a bit too big to kill," He said, catching his breath.

"Bloody hell, you are going to kill all its babies and leave it alive to grieve? What if it has more to revenge attack us while we sleep? Go back in and kill it. I don't want that wandering around the house... But hold your breath."

Ronan returned from his murderous trip back inside the house, coughing and spluttering again, which we both continued to do all the way home in the car.

"We should have taken the bottle home in case one of us has to go to hospital with poisoning," I said, thinking practically. "They always say that in first aid books, bring the bottle of stuff you drank."

"Well, I'm not going back in to get it. And we didn't drink it."

"It feels like I've drunk it, the smelly taste is still in my throat." I was coughing again, trying to rid myself of the yuck factor. "I don't think we should go back to the house for a few weeks."

"Yes, I think you are right. It's too tempting to do stuff," he said, still rubbing his eyes between splutters.

"I was thinking because we might get poisoned. To let the fumes subside. What the hell was that, anyway? And why the

33

hell did you stick your nose in the bottle?"

"Because I didn't know what was inside," he said, as if that explained it perfectly.

"That's exactly why you shouldn't have done that. And what were you thinking pouring it all over the floor when it's been sitting there for over ten years with a warning poison sign on the label?"

"To kill the eggs," he screeched back at me.

"We don't even know if they were eggs, it could have been just dust."

I was so good at 'I told you so's' when in hindsight.

"Are you seeing yellow spots before your eyes and is everything sounding echoey?"

"Christ no!" I said.

"No, neither am I," he smirked, pulling into the supermarket carpark. "I'll get you a bottle of red. It will stop the yellow spots from appearing."

While he was in the shop, I became increasingly aware of how sick I was feeling, but it wasn't the poison causing it, it was probably the large lump of tension gathering in my stomach as I tried to figure out how we would explain ourselves to the poisons unit should we get worse. "We were in our house... well, it's not our house... pulling a sink off the wall and demolishing the tiles... Basically vandalising a house that isn't ours."

I wondered at what point they would call the cops and have us arrested and deported. For a fleeting moment, I thought we should just make a run for the border then and there.

Ronan returned with the makings of a big salad and lemon chicken. It's something we have become used to in Italy, using lemon instead of gravy on chicken, especially in the summer.

"That wine you like was down to €2.20 a bottle, so I got you three."

"That will hopefully last me until we can go back to the killing fields."

In Ireland, the cheapest bottle of wine I'd buy was €14. Here I balk if a bottle of wine is over €5. A top shelf bottle of Barolo is €26. But the best bargain you can get is going into the local wine shop where you can get a five-litre jug filled by a hose of a decent house wine for less than a tenner.

The wine helped kill the poisonous smell and thoughts that evening, and we stayed away from the house for three weeks until we became the proud owners of the poison smelling cockroach-ridden derelict house.

I bought some dodgy looking cockroach killing spray, just in case there had been an invasion in our absence. We proceeded in with caution. The sulphur toxic smell had eased greatly. I did a Google Translate of the label of ant killer powder.

It was supposed to be diluted to a much weaker capacity and not just dumped into a puddle of water. There was nothing about toxic fumes. But then again, they probably didn't expect anyone to be stupid enough to use it after ten years. But they – the ghosts of Christmases past – hadn't met us.

5

MONTHLY PHONE CREDIT: €10

The first thing we do when ownership is declared is to call a meeting with the project manager, the architect, the builder, electrician, the plumber and carpenter.

Their arrival is like taking a walk through the duty-free fragrance section in an airport. Mixes of Eternity for Men, Hugo Boss and other expensive aftershaves and fragrances I don't know the name of, excite my nostrils even through my mask. Those who aren't wearing crisp shirts are rippling under perfectly pressed t-shirts and even though the barbers aren't open for business yet after lockdown, their hair is groomed to perfection.

We no longer want estimates, we want actual prices of what the work is going to cost, what has to be done and to emphasise that we need to be in by November, but we secretly mean Christmas.

A Rosie Life In Italy 2

"November what year?" laughs Tomo, our new project manager, although his job is really translator and communicator. I don't laugh back.

"We don't have a choice. Our lease is up at the end of November, but for his own reasons, Giovanni needs us out before Christmas. We are not prepared to rent somewhere else. Trying to find somewhere temporary that will accept two dogs and two cats is one issue, but the main issue is we just can't. We just don't have the budget for it. Our only other solution is to move back to Ireland and return next year when things are better, but please help us not to let that happen."

We've been in Italy three years but we haven't lived in Italy three years. We came here in a hurry and we have basically lived our Irish life from Italy, stuck behind our computers in our home offices, communicating with friends and family back home online. It's not that we are unsociable, we just have no opportunity to break in through the shell, we're not social butterflies and it has probably taken me the three years to get over the shock of moving here. We haven't integrated; we have bobbed in our inflatables around the perimeter, it's now time to fall in.

Before moving to Italy I had imagined that after six months, I would be fluent in Italian, sitting in piazzas having banter with the locals who would all know us by name and be calling in for a glass of vino and having us over for their big chaotic family dinners after we helped them with their grape and olive harvesting. Instead, I wasn't able to string a sentence together and the only Italian we really knew was Lucia, who refused to speak Italian to us. "No, it is too hard.

We speak English. I cannot switch to speaking Italian to you, it is unnatural."

And instead of helping with harvests, we have helped her fix toilets and unblock sinks in her agriturismo from time to time when she has an emergency.

We tried private Italian classes as a family. The teacher understood very little English; the idea being that it would force us to speak Italian. We all are at different levels of learning ability, so while the kids absorbed the words like sponges, Ronan and I struggled. I get caught up in trying to get the structure and grammar correct while Ronan feels hand gestures and adding 'o' to the end of any word will get him through any situation in Italy.

It all went downhill after the second or third lesson when we should have known by then how to ask questions; What is your name? Where are you from? Where do you live? etc. During the class, the teacher gave us time to practice asking each other the questions. Then near the end of the class the Italian she said, "You can ask me any questions?"

Ronan took this literally, "Which eggs in the supermarket are free range?"

It was something that had been bothering him every time he went to the supermarket. I could only stare in disbelief, but it took Luca and Izzy about two days to recover from the pains in their sides from laughing. They gave up on us after that and found their own sources to learn the language, Luca being the most consistent as he would need it for college, while I dabbled in online apps.

A Rosie Life In Italy 2

So when people ask me how long I have been in Italy, I say six months; I am too embarrassed to admit I am ignorantly living in their country longer than that without being able to communicate in their beautiful language.

To save any misunderstanding during the renovation process, I look for someone who can act as project manager. Not everyone needs a project manager, but we need someone who can speak very good English and fluent Italian and can keep things moving along and within budget by fighting our corner in contract negotiations and ensure everything stays within budget. Someone with contacts in the trade is a bonus.

Lucia recommended Tomo to us, "He's the best."

He's a smiley young guy who was training to be a geometra and then got sidetracked by running a bicycle shop. There's a picture of him holding a big fish in his contacts profile pic. I'm not sure what Lucia thinks he is the best at, perhaps fishing or fixing bicycles, as he has never project managed before, but we didn't have any other choices at the time and his English was good, he seemed to have good contacts and understand what we needed him to do. We had heard the stories of builders and tradespeople going AWOL halfway through the project, and Tomo assures us that this won't happen with any of the people he brings to the table.

Of course his name is not Tomo, it is Tommaso. I have 'Irishized' all the names of the workers for my Dublin tongue to get around. The same goes for Michele. We pronounce it Mick Kelly. There is also Damo (Damiano), Anto (Antonio), several Marios and Marco... well they don't change, they stay Marco and Marios.

It's better this way, for everyone's sakes, otherwise Ronan tries to pronounce the Italian version of names and Tommaso somehow ends up being called Tomatosauce-o and Fabricio ends up as Fabric-Conditioner.

On the first visit, they all spread throughout the house like monkeys let loose in a fruit market. We watch them measuring, discussing, staring at the hole in the roof, shouting – which is a friendly conversation in Italy – and then they all leave in their cars with notes taken to prepare quotes. Miraculously, none have touched any part of the house other than with their soles of their shoes. They leave as crisp and shiny as they have arrived. Unlike us. We just have to look inside the house and we get instantly covered in cobwebs and grime.

"So, what is the first step?" I ask Tomo, who seems excited by his new part-time role.

"You have to wait for the house to be officially registered in your names. Then we need to apply for the water to be connected and the utilities to be registered in your names. Work on the house cannot start until this is done."

"How long will that take?"

"I don't know, it depends." He doesn't explain any further. This will be the first of many 'it depends' answers I get. I have no idea if the renovation will take four months or four years because 'it depends.' What 'it depends' on, most of the time, is Italian bureaucracy; 'it depends' on how bothered the person is, who opens the file.

No one wants to take responsibility for anything when it comes to paperwork in Italy. Everything has to go through a process of being passed from Billy-o to Jack-o with multiple signatures and forests of paper.

"If something goes wrong down the line, the person who made the decision can go to prison. It is to stop the mafia interfering like they did in the past," Lucia explains. "It is crazy and stops business progress in this country so much. Italy spends millions each year in bureaucracy tactics to stop mafia interference and, in so doing, costs the country millions more in hindering entrepreneurship and stalling progress. This is why they will not respond by email or text. Everyone requires a meeting over the stupidest things because they don't want to write anything that they can be held responsible for."

"What about the 110% bonus system?" This was something widely talked about before we took anyone on, and everyone seemed very excited about it. It's a new eco bonus scheme to encourage people to upgrade their houses and to stimulate work within the construction industry in Italy.

"No one knows anything about how to apply for it. It is being advertised everywhere, but there are no details of what is required to apply for it. It seems very complicated and you would need to raise the energy rating of the house up by two levels," explains Tomo, trying to look serious.

"Surely an insulated roof, or just any roof without a gaping hole and windows with glass in them will raise the level?"

"They require you to change the heating system. As there is no heating system, you cannot change it," says Tomo, throwing an obstacle in the way. I wished I had fluency in

Italian. I am good at figuring ways to make things work and to fit things into the boxes they need to be fitted.

"There is a heating system," I say.

"No, there isn't." It is like he is suddenly putting barriers in the way of us applying for it.

"There is..." I argue. "There is a kerosene boiler on the third floor."

"You don't have a third floor."

"Yes, we do." I'm beginning to think we are talking about two different houses.

"You have a ground floor, a first floor and a second floor."

I don't know if it's just me or my Irish brain that labels them first, second and third storeys.

"You say tomAtoes I say tomato-es."

He's looking at me, confused again.

"On the top floor, we have a kerosene boiler." I note to myself to adjust to the Italian way and call the house levels; ground, first and second floors rather than three storeys.

"Oh yes, now I know what you are talking about. That might pass as acceptable to change... But you will also need to wrap the whole of the outside of the house in insulation."

"And cover the lovely brickwork?"

"Yes."

"Emm, no, that won't be happening."

A Rosie Life In Italy 2

"Maybe if you wait one year, then we will know how to apply or how it will work." He can see by my tightening lips that this is not an option. "There is an easier bonus scheme to apply for which gives you 50 percent back of what you spend."

"Well, that sounds good. What do we need to do for that?"

"I don't know. I don't know anyone that has yet applied for it. But I know you will need to make payments through an Italian bank."

"I wish you had told me about this before I paid the deposit to the builder."

Tomo shrugs and goes back to smiling.

I do the research into the scheme as best I can. The scheme is to promote work in the construction industry. Great, I can give them lots of work. They reimburse you over a ten-year period through your tax payments. That's not so good. However, a builder can buy the credit and get the reimbursement through their company.

Tomo is slow to respond to texts, not a good start to our working relationship. So I go ahead and I talk to Anto, our builder, by text using Google Translate, to see if he can do the reimbursement scheme. He looks into it, but is not keen.

"It is complicated. But if you find a way, I will try."

I continue to do Tomo's job for him and do my research.

In the meantime, following Tomo's advice, I go to open an account at a bank he recommends as the best and most friendly bank he has found. I feel it would be a good move anyway to establish my credit history here and for paying bills. I have an appointment with the director of the small, quiet bank near the train station. It's technically in Tuscany, as we are living on the border. The director seems very nice but can't talk a word of English. My Italian banter doesn't go beyond the weather, so ends quickly.

He has a retro flip calendar on his desk, the one where you click the bottom on the end to change the date.

It triggers a memory of my sister having the same one in the 70s and she'd let me press the button to change the date. I had left the memory of this flip calendar in the 70s and here it was, ta-da! I suddenly find myself welling up at the thought of my sister Eileen and need to distract myself, so I talk about the weather again. The conversation ends after a few nods and words. I won't be getting to practice any Italian here.

Twenty minutes into silent form filling, he asks me for my phone number. I give him my business card with my Irish number on it.

"Ah no, you need an Italian phone number to complete the registration for opening a bank account in Italy," he says in Italian several times before I understand.

So I go to a mobile phone network shop I find on Google Maps. It's a half hour car trip away in Perugia. I choose a package; we start to fill out the form and get to the part of a bank account. I give my Irish account.

"You need an Italian bank account to get a phone number," says the smiley guy behind the counter.

"But I need a phone number to open an Italian bank account?"

A Rosie Life In Italy 2

"I can see that this will be a problem for you." He is still smiling. No solution is offered.

"How about giving me a 'monthly 'top up' package that isn't attached to a bank account?"

"Okay, that could be a solution!"

Armed with my new Italian number, I make a new appointment at the bank. Two hours and a lot of silence, paper and signatures later, I have my Italian bank account opened. It only took two trips and nearly three hours.

I'm texting Tomo for an update on the utilities and he responds a week later. "I have applied for the water to be connected and I have also found out you will have to make payments by going into the bank and for them to fill out a special form. You can't make payments online and any payments made without the special form cannot be claimed for."

"That is inconvenient." I had a deposit invoice for the architect to pay so I went to the bank with my prepared words to say I want to pay with the benefit scheme.

"No, sorry we do not do that," says the teller at the bank when I tell them I want to pay using the Renovation Scheme Bonus.

I call Tomo. "The bank says they do not do it. I think they are misunderstanding me."

"You are saying it correctly, but not all banks do the credit scheme."

"But the bank you sent me to does, right?"

"No, it doesn't."

"So being with this bank is useless?"

"It is a very nice bank."

"But if I want to do the bonus scheme, I can't do it from that bank?"

"No."

"So I will need to use a different bank?"

"Yes, for the bonus scheme you will need to find a bank that will do it."

"Do you know one?"

"No."

I'm biting my tongue. I remind myself that banking advice was not part of Tomo's job brief, he was just giving me a friendly recommendation. This was something I would need to look into by myself, so I contact a commercialista I find through a social media group who is very helpful.

"The way the scheme refunds you the money is through tax decreases over ten years."

"But I won't be paying enough of tax to cover that?"

"There is another way... You need to find a bank that will buy the credit from you. You pay for everything, then they apply for the credit and they give you back 40 percent and the bank keeps ten percent. And it is possible to do it as non-resident. I will send you the clause number of the directive about this which you can give to your bank."

A Rosie Life In Italy 2

So the hunt is on to find an 'early adopter' bank that will do it. Luckily, with Mick Kelly's help, we find one. Just up the road, on the corner beside the pizzeria. The director is young and charismatic, he's a go-getter. He has all the info pack with highlighted marks in front of him when I arrive for our meeting with Tomo in tow.

I ask questions. He talks a lot. Tomo talks a lot. And the resulting reply I get is usually three words. He said no. He said yes. Why do Italians have to add so many words to what they are saying to a simple question?

He is perplexed about how I can apply as a non-resident, but he soon has the clause printed out that I give him the reference of. He is happy to do it if we give him full instructions on how it can be done, as he does not have time to look into it all. I agree to do his job for him.

I'm introduced to the only teller in the bank. Roberta. Roberta turns out to be a saint. She patiently opens up a new account for me in record speed of 1.5 hours with the help of a younger woman in the bank who speaks some English and enjoys the opportunity to practice it. She had spent a summer in Dublin as a student, and it was the best summer of her life. The only other person in the bank is 'Veronica' who seems to look after loans and mortgages. Veronica has the only other office next to the Director's. The younger woman suggests we meet to exchange conversation to help each other. I agree that would be great. I never see her again. I thought she worked at the bank but she was only a customer, calling in about something quick and spent over an hour of her time acting as translator to help a complete stranger set up their account.

I not only get a bank account opened but I get a deposit paid to the plumber who gave me his invoice the day before. He sends a text back 'She has already paid!!' and some party emojis. It wasn't meant for me. He sends me an apology for sending it to the wrong person. But I get from it that nobody expects to be paid on time, which is not how I work, so I feel they are all going to be happy campers.

I'm feeling positive again. The first thing that is needed on site is water and electricity. Tomo has sent in the application for the water to be connected, so all we can do now is to wait.

6

HALF LITRE OF GLOSS PAINT: €16

Two weeks go by and we still have not received a quote for the building work from Anto. The quote will arrive via Mick Kelly's architectural approval along with Tomo's translating service.

"The roof will need repairs. Possibly you will need a new roof," Mick Kelly had told us after our first inspection visit with him before we committed to buying the house.

"How much will that cost?"

"About 26k," he suggested.

I thought that was a reasonable price until a friend of a friend in a supermarket after we had bought the house, asked us "What price did they quote you for the roof? I bet it was 20 to 26 thousand?"

"Yes, how did you know?"

"Because that is what they always say. You just wait and see, it will be a lot more than that."

I increase the amount of texts to Tomo chasing him for the builder's quote. I thought he was just ignoring me again, but after a three-week wait, when a meeting is called with us, Anto, Tomo and Mick Kelly, I realise why it took so long. A twenty-page document is waiting for us, outlining each element of the project. Each element is at least two paragraphs long. A new roof is included in the quote.

"But we don't need a new roof, do we? It just needs the hole patched up."

"It depends."

There are those words again.

"We won't know until we strip it back. If the beams are okay, then we do not need to do a new roof. But this is the cost if it does and it is important to be prepared for the worst and work back from that." The price for the roof alone is exorbitant; €65,663.98

I am using my translation app and realise it's for a very nice roof, one with new tiles and chestnut angled beams and chestnut-lined ceilings.

"Okay, first; we can use the old tiles from the roof."

Mick Kelly agrees that yes, that is possible. That knocks a small chunk off.

"And second, this is on the third floor so no one is going to see the pretty beams, so can we do it in cheaper wood and have plasterboard ceilings?" It takes a while to explain what I am trying to say and for it to sink in. Mick Kelly looks disappointed, as architects do when you tell them you have no appreciation for the finer details of their craft.

"We could do it in pine."

"That's if it is needed. Can we first assess if a new roof is needed? And I'd like a finish date to be set with penalties to be paid for any week it goes beyond. I want to move in on the 1st of November so they need to be finished by 31st of October." In my head I have built in a two-week slush fund of time, if they are out by mid-November it would give time for a good clean up before I start on the Christmas decorations, ready for Izzy's arrival back and for us to all move into the house together.

His eyebrows lift and he asks the same question Tomo had asked, "which year?"

I'm getting tired of it. "Are you saying they cannot finish the roof, electrics and plumbing in ten weeks?"

"Yes, but not complete the entire house."

"No, it will probably take us five years to finish the entire house. We just want these guys to do the roof, the electrics and plumbing and finish within ten weeks."

I don't think it has struck them that we intend to do a lot of the finishing work ourselves and over time. I'll soon find out that women doing DIY is not a common thing in Italy.

We discuss everything else in detail. It is all a moveable feast at the moment, but we sign on the dotted line to take Anto on as the builder for the project. He's a good guy and keen to get started. Each stage of the project will be agreed and priced before they carry the work out. The first thing we need is for the scaffolding to go up and this needs to be booked in.

I'm in the car with Ronan driving back to our rental, which brings us past the house.

"To date, no one has gone into the upper attic space to see if the beams are okay. They've all arrived in their Sunday best clothes, smelling gorgeous. No one has assessed the roof properly and yet they are just presuming we need a new roof. The house is dry. I am sure there is no need for a complete new roof," I say, surprising myself at complaining about the workmen looking fabulous, but I'm beginning to think they don't like getting their hands dirty.

"I've an idea." Ronan pulls into the garden of the house and takes a crowbar out of the back of the car. I don't ask why he has a crowbar in the back of the car. All I know is that it's been there for ages, forgotten about since our move from Ireland.

I follow him into the house and get distracted by visiting a piece of furniture I have been thinking about in one of the rooms; a laminate table from the 1960s. I had noticed something about it and had been thinking about it since our last visit. I soon realise it is as how I thought; a pasta making table complete with a pull-out flouring area and pasta roller in the side to hang the pasta on to dry.

I soon hear crashing and banging coming from upstairs. I take two steps at a time up to see what the hell has happened. Ronan is standing on a ladder and reefing down the plasterboard ceiling in the top room that already has the gaping hole.

"That should do it. They can have a better view of the beams now. It's tougher than I thought as it's not plasterboard, it's a mesh with a thin layer of a concrete mix in it," Ronan says, panting a little as a large flap of ceiling hangs from a beam while other chunks lie demolished on the floor.

He's covered from head to toe in grey dust, but unlike the others, he's not wearing his Sunday best. In fact, Ronan is in constant work clothes even when we are not renovating. He owns 27 shirts, but I've never seen him wear one of them, except when he is working at a wedding, which won't be happening again anytime soon.

He brushes off a spider half the size of his hand. "The beams look fine to me, except for that one." He points to the one that has taken the full brunt of the weather coming in through the hole in the roof above.

But then we notice each beam is meticulously carved and fitted into a complicated structure which has formed a rain-tight hat on our grand old lady for 100 years. It looks intricate, but we can see that no beam seems uniform. I already realise this is not good.

To replace one will have a knock-on effect on the next. It might be okay if we didn't have to put an iron band around the whole top where the roof meets the wall to make the house seismically compliant. This will involve taking the beams down and putting them back into place. It will be like trying to build the Taj Mahal out of matchsticks.

I am not grumbling about the need for a seismic band, which to me sounds like an enormous pair of elasticized knickers to keep our old dear's belly in while she's trying to look good in a tight dress. I really would prefer the third storey to stay in place should there ever be an earthquake in this non-earthquake zone.

"I think our old lady is going to need a new hat to go with her elasticized knickers."

Ronan solemnly nods in agreement. He knows exactly what I am referring to.

"I'll message Tomo and ask him to get that elusive engineer we have talked about so much out here to see what needs to be done."

There isn't a whole lot of DIY we can get started on until the builders have done their stuff, other than clearing out cobwebs and unsalvageable or reusable laminated chipboard furniture which hasn't stood the test of time like their more ancient, solid wood roommates left behind. There is a lot of knocking tiles and plaster off bellied walls, and sweeping and destroying. We are good at destroying.

Walking onto the second-floor balcony off the small room next to the room where Ronan has just demolished the ceiling, I notice the first bloom on one of the two giant magnolia trees that stand guard at the gates.

"First day of June and first bloom." This balcony will be one of my favourite spots in the house as it feels like a tree house with the birds so close in the top branches.

"Help me grab this pair of shutters, I can start working on them back home," I say to Ronan as I try to brush off some of the spider nests embedded between the slats of the weathered and wobbly shutters, before we unhook them from their hinges.

"Home? You mean here or Ireland?"

"I mean Giovanni's place, where we have electricity and water. I am hardly going to bring these back to Ireland whenever that happens again. This is going to get confusing, isn't it? How about we refer to this house as the work house and Giovanni's as home for now?"

"The Workhouse?!" Ronan is laughing as he knows I meant 'the house we were working on' and not 'The Workhouse', which would have had very negative connotations for our great grandparents during the Famine in Ireland.

"I like it! The Sighing House has now become The Work House. I'll get it made on a plaque."

"No! It's a temporary name until Christmas. After that, when all the hard labour is finished, we will need to think of a prettier name for our old lady."

I have counted 33 windows, which add up to 66 window frames, 66 outer shutters and 66 inner shutters. That is 231 pieces of woodwork to be washed, sanded, undercoated and painted with two coats. That's a lot of paint and sandpaper.

So we venture to the big warehouse DIY store. It's the first time I have experienced more than ten people at any one time in the last three months. It is nice to feel normal again for a moment, but then I remind myself we are not back to normal, the virus is still here. We just have to be cautious and considerate of others and live with it.

Everyone is wearing a mask. The previous day Umbria only recorded 60 new cases of COVID-19 in a population of 890k, but after about 15 minutes I'm breathing faster and even though there is air conditioning my skin is starting to feel clammy and warm enough to sweat. I find Ronan standing in the centre aisle looking for me.

"Rosie, let's get out of here. There are too many people for my liking."

"Same," I respond as we grab a variety of pots of paint, paintbrushes, sandpaper and cleaning stuff and leave as quickly as possible.

We go back 'home' to Giovanni's, our rental twelve minutes' drive away from our renamed Sighing House. Giovanni's place looks majestic on the outside, painted that dark pink colour common in Italy. We called it the Barbie house for a while when we first arrived. It stands in the centre of four fields. Half of one field is set out as a garden with a rose and lilac lined driveway and olive and fruit trees sprinkled around the lawn. The other fields are used for crops, sometimes wheat or barley, and sometimes chickpeas.

The fields across the road between the house and Lake Trasimeno are annually rotated between chickpeas and sunflowers. This year is a sunflower year for the fields closest to us.

I set up a workstation on the terrace and start my mission. First, sanding off the chipped paint. The weather over the last God-knows-how-long-since-they-were-painted-last years has got rid of most of the outer gloss green for me, so the sanding doesn't take long. Next, the undercoat.

I stir the tin and begin. It's like flour mixed with water. Absolute crap. Luckily I only bought one tin of it, but the work on the shutters will have to stall until I can get a different tin of undercoat. I'm secretly glad as it lets me skip to my favourite evening thing to do which is sit out on the terrace with a glass of Chardonnay and look out across the heads of the olive trees and beyond the sea of yellow-faced sunflowers and watch the lake change colour between light blue, to pink and gold.

When there is a full moon, the lake turns silver, but when the moon is not so bright, the terrace is perfect for stargazing. Or sometimes we go and lie in the grass in front of the woodshed where we have an uninterrupted view of the bright constellations with the heavy scent of jasmine in the air. This is the one thing I will miss about this house. The countryside feeling and privacy in the evenings once Giovanni has gone home from working in the fields. At our new place we have a relatively busy road in front of the house, neighbours on both sides and a train-line at the end of the garden between us and the path around the lake.

But we have had enough of being cut off from the world. Having an idyllic lakeside walk into a lively town and a train station is worth sacrificing the stargazing for. I add a note to my garden ideas list; 'build a stargazing platform somewhere'.

This evening is the first of many that we return home cobwebbed and a little overwhelmed by the tasks ahead. I pour a second glass of crisp white and sit on the terrace watching a hummingbird hawk moth hover in front of the first sunflower to show her face. They are from the seeds I planted at the start of lockdown and hoped the pandemic would be over by the time they bloomed. COVID-19 is not over, but things are moving on.

Over the next few days we go through four different brands of undercoat. We discover paint is hit and miss in Italy, but mostly really crap. Eventually I find one that does what it says on the tin and I get one shutter done and I feel accomplished. Paint isn't cheap either. At €16 per pot, I calculate one pot will do 1.5 shutters. I calculate in the car home that equals to 22 pots of paint, which will cost €352 for top coats, never mind the undercoat. It also takes three days to finish one shutter. That's 99 days if I do nothing else. I've a feeling I am going to hate the sight of these shutters very soon.

7

BURRATA: €7

Several times in the last six months, I have been a blubbering mess. It comes over me all of a sudden, but is usually triggered by a phone call. I go and find solitude somewhere, close a door or stand behind a tree and let the wave of deep sadness escape in silent giant sobs.

It is not because of the house renovations or delays, it is the 'not-knowing' that the pandemic has caused. The not-knowing of when I'll see my parents again and the not-knowing when I will see our daughter again. Twenty-three years previously, at the age of 24, I gave birth to my best friend on the feast day of Saint Nicholas. Before the lockdowns, the longest we had ever been apart was four weeks, and that was torture. It had now been more than five long months. The first two months apart were expected, as she was working in London, but then COVID hit.

Today I am not blubbering. I am smiling. I always have a big smile on my face after buying fresh Burrata in Italy as I feel like I've won the goldfish at the village fair. The fresh creamy stracciatella that bursts out of the pearly white encased pouch of mozzarella, which goes perfectly with my fig chutney, is presented bobbing in a bag of water. I feel I should take it home and release it into a pond.

Today the smile planted on my face is bigger than ever, as Burrata is Izzy's favourite thing to eat and I am buying it for her arrival tomorrow. After three months of solitary lockdown in the UK, she is coming back to Italy with no return date set. I didn't allow myself to get excited until I received the text from Ronan at Rome airport "Got Her!" She was in the car with her Dad who drove solo to pick her up as Italy's pandemic rules state only two people allowed in a car at any one time.

There's no sign of vaccines yet and, as Ronan is diabetic, we are taking all the precautions. This includes him not being allowed to hug Izzy when she arrives, which I knew would be the hardest part. He had to wait outside the air terminal. No hugging on arrival, especially after she hadn't had physical contact with anyone for three months, is tough.

Even when your child is 23 years old, they are still your baby and you want to hug them and kiss them better. But as we had got this far in the pandemic with none of us getting sick through isolation and unable to see family, we cannot risk it all now.

We had all agreed how we would do it. Once she was here, she would stay in isolation in the separate apartment for the first week. When with us she would stay masked up, wear plastic gloves, we'd disinfect surfaces, and she'd have her own set of dishes and cutlery. This was from all the pieces of advice we had read.

A Rosie Life In Italy 2

While Ronan went to pick her up, I had an idea. "Luca, we could make hug suits, out of garbage bags."

Within an hour, we had created three full suits of armour from plastic bags, clear plastic from a business folder for our face screen, plastic sleeves and rubber kitchen gloves. There was no way the virus could get through it and wearing our suits we could both jump on her and squeeze her tight until Ronan got into his and could take over squeezing the life out of her.

"We could make these and sell them. Covid hug suits, fun for all the family," said Luca while embellishing his suit with wool hair and horns made from toilet roll tubes.

Each morning and evening for the next week, I put on my hug suit and gave her a long-missed hug. We kept our distance otherwise, lounging in the garden, chatting. Once the first week was over and neither she or us were showing any symptoms of COVID, we turned the suits back into garbage bags and we held each other like koalas whenever we were in the same room.

It was after about day ten she broke the news that she had a flight booked back to the UK in two weeks' time.

"Two weeks? Why so soon? You can't go. What if it all goes crazy again?"

"I've met someone. A guy. I really like him."

"How the hell did you get a boyfriend during lockdown?"

"I knew him from before. We had been texting while we were both in isolation. And then when Britain lifted restrictions a couple of weeks ago, we got together for a few social distancing walks and well... the rest is now history."

Why it couldn't have happened ten weeks ago and saved us all the tears and anxiety rather than just a week before she left to be with us will forever be a mystery. But what was clear was she had a life now. There. Away from us. Things were opening up in the UK. Her friends were starting to return to their jobs. She was moving into a new apartment and now she had a boyfriend, someone I had to share her with.

The grief of waiting and worrying all of April and May still has a hold on me. Three weeks, including a week of physical distancing, just felt too short. Two more weeks of bliss passed, sitting on the sofa watching trash and eating trash. It was background noise to our nattering. The guys preferred to stay away from these sessions, but joined us in the evening for a family movie and food.

I really try to focus on enjoying the time we have while she is here. There isn't anywhere we can go, but we are all happy to stay at home in our cocoon together. If it had been like this with her here throughout lockdown, and my Mam and Dad, I wouldn't have cared how long it went on for.

But it wasn't. If it all had happened a year later, things would have been so different. We would have had the house finished, Izzy's job would have been more established. My Mam and Dad would have moved over as planned in September. But that is all now put on hold. It terrified me to think how long it might be before I get to see my parents and I now wonder if they will ever get to move to Italy where I can wrap them in cotton wool and look after them for the rest of their days.

I know my Dad has reservations about moving to Italy because of the food. He is a typical 85+ year old Irish man who likes his potatoes. His opening line for every phone call is "Are you eating macaroni?"

Macaroni was one of our only few experiences of 'Italian' food when we were growing up. At the weekend, as an evening treat, we'd have macaroni with warm milk and sugar or semolina with jam to fill us up before bed. I loved stirring in the raspberry jam dollops, turning the pale yellow pudding into a raspberry pink colour.

Tinned spaghetti hoops in tomato sauce on toast for lunch was another Italian favourite. I was about nine when my Mam starting to buy frozen things called 'pizzas'. They came in five packs and were small frozen disks of dough with a scraping of tomato sauce and a sprinkling of grated cheese across the top. These were my experiences of Italian cuisine growing up in Ireland during the 70s.

Ronan's experiences of Italian cuisine growing up were equally scarce. He claims he was one of the first people to experience pizza in Ireland. There is an entire culture of Italian owned fish and chip shops in Ireland – so much so that we all thought it was the national food of Italy. Ronan was friendly with a local Italian chipper owner and one evening, back in the early 80s, Ronan stopped off at the chipper on the way home from the pub and the owner was very excited. He was having a thing called a 'pizza oven' delivered the following week. "YOU have to come and experience the pizza."

"What is it?"

"It is like'a... bread... with eh... the cheese melted on top."

"So, a toasted cheese sandwich?" said Ronan, waiting on his Italian fish and chips.

"No, it is different. Come and see next week."

Ronan was there for the opening launch of the pizza oven. He wasn't that impressed and told his friends; "It's basically a roundy cheese sandwich with no bread on top, I can't see it taking off."

My parents were due to move over for the winter as soon as the Workhouse was ready, but the pandemic has them staying put in Ireland. I think my dad is getting cold feet about ever moving to Italy now. "Are you eating macaroni?" is often followed by, "So what are the pubs like where you live? Can you have an ol' sing song in them?"

"There are no pubs as we know them in Italy. There are bars, they sell coffee and the old men gather there to play cards."

I can see he's not attracted to this idea, so I try to paint a picture more in-keeping with what he has in mind. "There are outdoor bars along the lake and they have a lot of festivals that have music. There are also a lot of English people we know here who would probably gladly meet up for a weekly singsong in the back garden."

Dad is miffed at the idea of there being no pubs in Italy. It could be a deal breaker, even though he hasn't been to a pub in years in Ireland.

As Izzy's date of departure gets closer, the deep sadness won't lift. The more I try to cover it, the worse it gets. I want to hug her constantly but can't. It's 33 degrees during the day here, so we're both too sweaty.

In 36 hours she'll be gone and I don't know when I'll see her again. If times were normal, I'd be okay, but there's a pandemic and I can't just hop on a flight and go visit her every six weeks like before. I keep telling her to pretend she'll come back in August to visit. We both know it won't happen. She's working during September and October so we won't see her then. November is close to Christmas, so she'll probably hold off until Christmas. That's a long time.

On the way to the airport, I put my hand back to hold hers like I used to do when she was in her car seat. She wouldn't sleep without me holding her hand and her comfort was pushing my cuticles back with her nails. It was annoying and sometimes painful, but it got her asleep. On the way to the airport, she unconsciously does it again. My eyes fill with tears and, in the middle of saying something, I begin to choke on my words, so I put on my sunglasses.

At the airport, there are barriers at the doors. We walk in the entrance and a guy asks, "Are you all travelling?"

"No. Only her."

"Only those travelling beyond this point."

There are only ten minutes before the gate is officially closed, so we have to rush. No long goodbyes, but extended hugs. Thankfully, there is no time to cry until I get back to the car. Usually I'm fine, but the pandemic restrictions are unpredictable for the future. What if travel ceases again between the UK and Italy? What if it all flares up again and she can't get back for Christmas? I can't let myself think like that.

What's really got at me though, is the realisation as this is how it now is. She has her life there and we have our lives here. There's no coming back to us for long stints between jobs anymore. She has a bigger life away from us, which she will miss whenever she is with us now. This is it. The umbilical cord has truly been severed. And my heart wants to break. But I won't let it.

I tell myself that I need to get a grip and stop being a wreck. She needs me to be strong and not fragile. I know she misses me too, she just has a handsome distraction now.

But so do I. I have the house. I'll throw myself into that, into making it a beautiful home that we'll all love and look forward to coming back to. It makes me more determined to create a perfectly styled Christmas at the house ready for her return.

"Should we go for a gold and red themed tree or silver and purple?" I contemplate on the way home. Ronan is looking at me like I am a bad smell again.

"Rosie I think we should get a roof and windows first?"

"I think we'll go for red and gold, it will be warmer looking," I say, ignoring him. I need to plan, it's the vision of the perfect Christmas in our house that will keep me from sinking during the coming months.

8

VINTAGE BOTTLE OF CHAMPAGNE: €40

Weeks go by. There is no way of hurrying up the water company. We are okay with waiting, as the previous owners have left rooms full of furniture and stuff that all needs to be cleared, sorted and assigned or thrown out, so we have plenty to do.

The first few visits are done with respect, creeping quietly around the house, like it's a sacred space belonging to someone else. I've been dreaming about what we would do as soon as we officially got ownership of the house, but now it feels different. Overwhelmingly different. The dream has become reality and I don't know how to move it from the floaty space to an actual 'this is really happening' physical reality.

We rummage around from room to room. In the downstairs front room there is the fascist-styled cabinet where 20 saucer champagne glasses waited with dust cocktails until Uncle Francesca spotted them and squirrelled them away for herself before we owned the house and its contents. She hadn't taken the bottle of unopened Moet champagne though.

The quote for the new roof comes in from the builder. I'm having a small heart attack. I need to either drink the champagne if it is not worth much or sell it to pay the four times difference of the original estimate. It will be negotiated, it will have to be negotiated.

We start working on clearing the old scary stuff, like the old kitchen cupboards.

In one of the kitchen cupboards I find a beveled glass oil and vinegar set from 1920s perhaps, judging by the design. The holder isn't real silver. I'll give it a clean-up and perhaps not use the vinegar left in it. There are hand blown glasses, racks of mismatched saucers and plates, cups and bowls. Tarnished cutlery and eight wooden spoons of different lengths and sizes.

I had asked the previous owners to tell me the history of the house and the people who lived there. They said it had a great history but didn't tell me anymore. So we're piecing it together from the things we find. There were three brothers and a sister living here until their old age. Each had their own apartment in the house. Each apartment tells a story. Miranda was the last to leave as I found a letter from her to the electricity company explaining she was 90 and living alone. This was a bit of a fib, as I know from the deeds she was 80 when we bought it and the letter is dated 15 years previously.

Her niece, who we named Uncle Francesca, was also 80, a month between them, according to the deeds. As Miranda

A Rosie Life In Italy 2

had Alzheimer's, Francesca was her power of attorney. It's in Miranda's sitting room we find the champagne and the glassware. Perhaps she was a party girl in her day. There are also religious medals and mementos. Folded wrapping paper and string. It reminds me of my grandmother, who threw away nothing that could be reused.

One of the brother's apartments was completely cleared out. Except for a large wooden gun cabinet with a box of lead shot. He was a hunter, which is common in this area. The other guy was the winemaker and gardener as the key to the shed and cantina is in his apartment. He had kids who grew into adults, moved on, cleared his place after he had passed on and had their own kids who now live in Milan and were one of the nine heirs we bought it from. I don't know which siblings the other six cousins who were in on the inheritance were related to, but I don't think any of them were direct descendants to the most interesting guy; Paolo Legume. The owner of the apartment which Luca and I have become fascinated with.

The initials PL above the front door in the iron fan light sit below the keystone with the build date; 1923. This was him, or perhaps he was named after his father and he owned the house initially; Paolo Legume. Legume means Bean. We have bought Mr Bean's house.

The bureau in the corner with its five wide drawers brimming with curiosities that had no other place to be but in a man drawer and five shelves above full of books is now mine and Lucas' go to place when we need a break from destroying and clearing stuff. The bureau to me is like finding a treasure box, a time capsule into the past of the house and the man behind the initials above the door.

We start with the top drawer. Wooden rulers, wooden set squares, letter stencils and pencil nibs explain he was into something that required precision drawing. Lettering, graphics.

Rolls of unused film, negatives, pieces of camera lenses, a camera instruction manual, an old light meter – Paolo was a keen photographer. With a love of art and photography, he's becoming more appealing to all of us.

And then Luca hits treasure. A small wooden box with Japanese lettering, a sliding lid about the size of a cigarette lighter, tucked away at the back, not hidden, just forgotten. I slide back the lid. Inside there is a long black stone with a carving of a man... a monk.

"What is it?" I'm rolling the stone between my fingers, but it doesn't feel like stone. It warms too quickly.

"I don't know but I know who will, time to ask a friend." Luca takes a picture with his phone and has it winging its way to Jo, an English friend that lives in Japan. Within an hour, we have a reply.

"It's definitely Japanese – the first two characters are 日本 = Nihon, meaning Japan. That's the easy bit... The kanji can be read as Nihon Buson, but it means nothing when you read it like that. The other way to read it is Yamato Takeru who was an emperor in 72AD – that's who the carving is."

A Rosie Life In Italy 2

In the meantime Luca is doing his own Google research and while I'm mallet-ing some bellied plaster off a wall downstairs, he comes in with what he discovered.

"It looks like solid ink used in calligraphy. You grind the inkstick as you need it. And Jo has got back... The writing on the side... see the character 堂 ?" he says, showing me something I can't see without my glasses and through the dust stuck to my eyelashes. "She thinks it is linked to a temple. Jo says, 'In Japan it is common to visit temples and get what they call an 'o-mamori' with the name of the temple written on it. It's a little fabric bag which contains something holy inside it, sometimes just a simple prayer. This one in your picture is not an 'o-mamori' but it could be a souvenir bought in a temple."

"Fascinating... now grab a mallet, there's work to be done."

As we both whack and chip away the loose plaster, we can't help but discuss Paolo. Had he been to Japan? Or perhaps someone had been there and given it to him. It would be an appropriate gift, considering his love of lettering and drawing.

"I found a flying manual too," says Luca as he steps out of the way of a large slab of plaster falling from a height, narrowly missing his head. "And something that looks like a dial off a plane and neatly drawn diagrams. Perhaps he was a pilot?"

"Well, that would make sense of the photo hanging in the hallway." I am referring to the framed black-and-white photo hanging on the wall downstairs of a crashed small plane in a vineyard with some people standing in front.

"Ha, you mean he wasn't very good at his job?"

"Maybe the house came with the job in the factory down the road?"

The town of Passignano had an aircraft factory. It built water planes. The buildings are still there; double-storey warehouses sandwiched between the road and the lake. Only the skeleton of metal girders stand now where there was once a roof. It's all fenced off waiting for someone to decide what to do with the ugly site that has historic significance. I heard Steven Spielberg, who owns a house in the hills, had considered turning it into film studios, but that could be just a rumour.

"That is a meter for measuring electrical currents. Those notes refer to how transistors work, judging from the drawings, they look like an electrical circuit drawing and an Ampere meter (A) the symbol at bottom of page looks like a 'diode' or a 'semi conductor' so he may have been an electrical engineer working with aircraft circuits?" informs one of my Facebook friends the following day, solving the mystery of the dial and drawings Luca found.

So Paolo was an electrical engineer who liked photography. The house was built around the same time as the water plane factory, so perhaps the house came as part of the job? Slowly, the jigsaw puzzle of Paolo is coming together.

There is a lot more stuff to get through in the drawers and shelves. It will take days, maybe weeks. But we still have time. There is no hurry on the water company and even though we are calling Tomo-who-answers-when-he-feels-like-it regularly, there seems to be no sign of the scaffolding arriving either.

9

ULTRASOUND SCAN: €60

"I think I need to go to a doctor. There's something weird happening to my stomach when I do a sit-up. Look at this," says Ronan lying on the bed beside me and does a sit-up. A pointy ridge depresses down the centre of his belly as his stomach muscles tighten.

I'm trying to not look too shocked, but I can't help myself. "Ronan, what the hell is that? It looks like an alien baby is about to burst through your skin."

"Ha ha, Rosemary's baby! Get it?!"

"Seriously, that looks serious."

"Yeah I Googled it, I think it's a herniated aorta or an aneurysm," he says, looking down at his alien invaded stomach.

"Don't be ridiculous, your aorta goes to your heart."

"It also goes down the centre of your stomach, do you not know anything?" He's delighted to be getting his own back for once on his know-it-all wife.

I'm immediately on my phone Googling "Where is Aorta?" and I get a small town in The Netherlands.

So I take a different route, cut to the chase and Google 'Aorta abdominal aneurysm' and read aloud what I find.

"An abdominal aortic aneurysm (AAA) is a bulge or swelling in the aorta, the main blood vessel that runs from the heart down through the chest and tummy. An AAA can be dangerous if it is not spotted early on. It can get bigger over time and could burst (rupture), causing life-threatening bleeding."

"You see, I told you it's in your stomach, you should believe me on these things, my grandparents were doctors."

His line "my grandparents were doctors" has been used throughout our years together when he's had to deal with things like retrieving a tiny bell Luca had stuffed in his ear, cuts, fractures, nose bleeds, my pregnancies, dog emergencies and basically anything that I would have felt leg wobbly about. He would deal with it, soothing everyone with the line, "Don't worry, I know what I am doing, my grandparents were doctors." Not that he ever met his grandparents or did any medical training, not even a first aid course.

"For God's sake, Ronan, that's life threatening. When did you notice this?"

"About a week ago."

A Rosie Life In Italy 2

"And you are only mentioning it now?" I'm still shocked that I didn't know the aorta ran through the stomach but also at Ronan's casualness over his life-threatening condition.

"I thought it would go away."

"What? You thought your aorta would go away?" I'm already texting Lucia, to ask her to help us make an appointment with a doctor and I explain why.

As we are not yet full residents in Italy, we have not been assigned a doctor and thankfully we have had no cause to go to one until now, other than me with my frozen shoulder.

Lucia is on it immediately and texts back, "I have an appointment made for later this morning with the doctor of my parents. She is a very good doctor. She is the best."

"Is it the same doctor you brought me to about my shoulder?"

"Yes, I have gone to her all my life. She will soon retire so she knows everything."

I have previously questioned Lucia's judgement of the doctor's worthiness, when she told me the three-choice prescription she gave to Lucia for stress. "You need to take up meditation or get a strong man to help you with the farm or take up smoking," was her verdict and advice.

When Lucia told me I quickly offered her a solution "Ronan is a meditation teacher, he can teach you," so she wouldn't seriously consider the last option.

We arrive at the surgery and take a ticket and wait to be called. She's an older, no-bullshit doctor, who doesn't speak

English, so Lucia has to come with us to our medical appointments until we get better at Italian.

When I asked about payment at the end of my frozen shoulder visit, the last time we were here, via Lucia, the doctor said to Lucia, "You can owe me lunch at your family's restaurant". It all seemed like a fair deal; I drag my Italian neighbour to be an unpaid translator and she then, in turn, gets to pay for my treatment by giving the doctor a free lunch.

Ronan lies on the doctor's treatment bed and illustrates the problem by doing a sit-up. Her first reaction, "Why are you do sit-ups? You are too old to be caring about a six-pack."

"Because I want to stay fit?"

She tuts. "It is not your aorta, it is your stomach muscles. They have detached and separated. You need to stop doing sit-ups. You will never have a flat stomach because of this. But I will send you for a scan anyway."

"So it is not life threatening?" I ask.

"No. Are you disappointed?" she smirks at me. Lucia is laughing all the way through while doing the factual translation.

"What causes it?" asks Ronan.

"Often pregnancy... but in your case probably lifting heavy objects."

A penny drops for me. "Oh my God... could that have happened to me during pregnancy? Does that explain why I haven't been able to get a flat stomach for the last 24 years no

A Rosie Life In Italy 2

matter how hard I try?" Not that I have actually tried that hard.

She looks at me over her glasses. "Yes, probably... it is too late now for you."

We leave the surgery with both of us written off as wrecks, doomed for Telly Tubby Land for all of eternity and with another promise of a free lunch for the doctor from Lucia.

She still hasn't taken advantage of the last free lunch, so I'm expecting her to arrive someday at the restaurant with a list of guests and the dates of our medical appointments beside each one she is owed a meal for.

"At least we know you are not going to explode," I say as we drive to the private medical clinic for Ronan's scan, which is just three miles down the road.

The clinic is a fantastic facility, modern, clean, no waiting. Ronan's scan confirms the doctor's prognosis and the prescription of:- No more sit-ups and, most of all, no heavy lifting. I wince; he's just silently prescribed me as a pain in the ass too.

We can live without Ronan doing sit-ups, actually we can both live happily with the thought of not being allowed to do a star jump, sit-up or any physical exercise again but no heavy lifting when we are about to embark on a massive renovation project?

Ronan doesn't mention it again, which means he is going to ignore the advice and I'm going to have to turn into the silently prescribed pain in the ass. The nagging wife who will constantly have to remind him every time I catch him carrying something heavy, which I feel will be often.

The technician has time, so he offers to scan Ronan's kidneys, liver and whatever else he finds – it's like when we go to the vet. She gives the pets a full checkup while we are there for no extra fee. And like our pets, Ronan gets a clean bill of health.

"Everything is looking good," the technician says in English, genuinely happy for Ronan or perhaps happy to get the opportunity to practice his English.

On the way home, we stop off in what will be our new hometown soon and buy gelato to celebrate Ronan not being pregnant with an alien baby, and both of us never having to do sit-ups again.

As Ronan was diagnosed as being type 2 diabetic about six years ago, gelato is a rarity. He usually picks an odd combination such as watermelon and coffee, while I prefer pistachio and coconut.

Pre-Covid, we would be back in Ireland every six weeks and would top up three months' supply of his various medications whenever we needed before returning to Italy. The 20 boxes of pills were interesting to explain whenever stopped going through airport customs, so we learned to carry a copy of his prescription with us.

One thing that has held us back from going full hog on residency in Italy is that we heard pharmaceuticals are expensive here. And thanks to the joys of COVID pandemic restrictions, we hadn't been able to get back to Ireland and his drug supply is running low.

A Rosie Life In Italy 2

"I brought my prescription with me from Ireland to show the doctor in case she needed it. Since we are in town, I think we should bite the bullet and try to get my prescription fulfilled here," Ronan says, slurping up the last of his watermelon gelato. I'd been at him to do this for months but he was reluctant as he knew how much this was going to cost unsubsidised, but the visit to the doctor probably gave him a wake-up call and he decided that his grandparents being doctors in the 1900s probably didn't qualify him to mess around with his medication any longer.

I went into the pharmacy instead of Ronan, as I had rehearsed what to say in Italian, and had taken €250 out of my bank ready for the bill we are expecting. I queue masked and gloved and, on my turn, enter the pharmacy and present the prescription sent from our doctor in Ireland.

She takes the prescription from me, enters it into the computer. After a moment, she pulls out drawers and filled a bag with three months' supply, which she hands to me.

My palms are sweating, causing the bundle of notes to stick to my hand. It is as if the cash felt it would be better spent on buying all the remaining paint needed for the shutters that month or a washing machine, rather than Ronan's medication. I'm standing there waiting on the verdict, thinking there were so many things we badly needed that this money could buy each month.

"That is €7 please," the pharmacist says in Italian. I'm sure I heard her wrong and hand her €80, expecting a tenner in change or a demand for more. She hands the cash back "No, no sette!"

I look at her, confused. She points at the single digit number on the cash register and nods a reassuring smile.

"His medication is subsidised here too? And even better than Ireland!" She has no idea what I just screeched from behind my mask. We could have been saving €4 each month by getting his medication here all this time.

I quickly add a hydrating facemask and a nice moisturiser that is on the counter display. I meet up with Ronan in the car park and hand him the new total of €48 that he owes me for being his drug runner and negotiator.

10

LINTEL: €471

Luca and I continue to sort out our Aladdin's cave, Paolo's room; boxing things we want to keep in grape crates and moving them across the hall to store in one of the bigger rooms, which will hopefully remain untouched should we need to remove the roof.

In the room, there is a gentleman's wardrobe. It was a piece I fell in love with when we viewed the house and I was relieved to see the old owners hadn't taken it. It's tagged to be one of the first things I will spruce up for our room as it is so pretty, with a long mirror on the door of the section for suits. On the inside of the door there is a hanger for neck ties which would be perfect for necklaces if I ever get around to dressing up again in something other than dusty old work clothes. The shorter shelved section has three drawers underneath and both sections have a small rectangular copper relief of roses above each door. Beside the wardrobe stands a wooden suit stand with a clasped trouser press. He wore suits. I find a box with three sets of Italian leather shoes and shoeshine. Mens.

European size 9. So he was not too tall, perhaps 5'8". Paolo liked to be well-presented.

Moving the books from the top shelf is daunting. I can't see what is above other than cobwebs. After at least 20 years of not being moved, the dust has formed a crust on the top of the full set of encyclopedias from 1933. Inside one, a telegram waiting to be written is used as a bookmark. I wonder if he ever got back to reading the page. These will be interesting to browse through on winter evenings after I learn Italian. I need a room for them.

Though treasure hunting in Paolo's room is madly interesting, there is work to be done. I leave Luca to it while I go downstairs and chisel away the plaster of the dividing wall between the kitchen and sitting room. Beneath the plaster there is another great redbrick wall, similar to the one we found in the guest kitchen.

"How about we make the front room into a Tranquilla Room?... A room without a TV or devices, somewhere to read and write?" I say as another slab of plaster falls to the ground.

Ronan agrees. He agrees to everything, as he knows I'll change my mind twenty more times before and after we are finished.

I stop short when I am halfway chiselling across the doorway. "Ronan, look... there's no lintel. I don't think this is a weight bearing wall. But the bricks above the doorway are resting on... nothing. The plaster seems to be keeping them together."

"Step slowly away from the plaster," Ronan says like I am holding a murder weapon over a dead body.

A Rosie Life In Italy 2

"That might not be a weight bearing wall... but those are," he says as we look at the cracks above the doorway from the sitting room and the blocked-up doorway from the kitchen to the hallway that we have knocked through and reopened. It's not a crack that has gone unnoticed before. My Dad and Mam always taught me to be wary of houses with cracks running up the walls above doorways.

"It only matters if the crack is showing through on the other side. The house has stood for 100 years. It will be all right," Mick Kelly said when I pointed it out during the viewing before we finally purchased.

Ronan gently taps away some of the plaster that has a crack running up it and then goes to the next one. "There are no lintels in either of these doorways."

We walk more gently around the rooms as we realise that the bricks above the doorways in the 100-inch-deep walls supporting the two stories above are being held together with plaster. I add 'lintels' to the 'urgent' list for the builder. It's a list that is getting longer.

With my miraculously floating red brick reveals on hold, we venture out to the overgrown garden to get away from the dust. "We still haven't explored the end shed," says Ronan, lighting up a cigarette.

"You mean the one that needed to be DESTROYED," I'm referring to our house buying meetings when the notary pointed out that there was no planning for the end shed and before we bought the house, the shed would need to be DESTROYED. The word 'Destroy' is used a lot when Italians are talking English when they could say 'knock it down' or 'demolished' or 'levelled out a bit'. The word is always said in quite a menacing voice. They used the word a lot during our house buying and planning, which gave the experience a touch of a Marvel episode.

"How about now?" I look at Ronan. We are both feeling brave. The end shed is divided into three. It covers half the width of the garden and is covered in thick ivy and brambles galore. We've gone as far as the door of each previously. The first was a work shed. There are boxes of the 'lovely' red tiles from upstairs, mint green subway tiles from one of the bathrooms, interior window shutters and what looks like a lot of electrical leftovers.

My bravery takes the form of accompanying Ronan to the door of the second section, which is divided lengthways in two by a cement brick wall. Beyond the wall there is no light other than the doorless doorway. There's an antique wooden ladder hanging the length of the wall. It will be perfect for jasmine to climb on. I pretend it's the brambles that are holding me back.

"I don't have long sleeves on. You go." Ronan goes even though he's also wearing a vest top. What is really stopping me is the shield of horror movie thick cobwebs curtaining the entrance to the back room.

"I think this was their wine cellar."

"For it to be a cellar, it needs to be under the house, I think?"

"Well, whatever it's called, the place where they make wine... the cantina. There are some of those glass demijohns down the back. And there's a barrel, should I look in it?"

A Rosie Life In Italy 2

I feel like we are on 'I'm a Celebrity Get Me Out of Here' and he's looking for the token that will feed us tonight but may have to plunge his hand into a barrel full of snakes to achieve the goal.

"Yes, of course, it might be full of gold."

"No, it's empty he calls out. But hang on... bloody hell."

"What is it?" I am thinking the worst; scorpions?

"There are bottles of wine. One, two, three, four... ten. Ten green bottles of vintage wine! All stored perfectly on their side. Bloody hell! We may have found a way to pay for all those lintels!" Ronan announces, making his way through the theatre-style curtain of cobwebs, holding a bottle in each of his hands like they are Oscars.

"Do you want to try one?" says Ronan, egging me on to open a bottle of the wine. Ronan has been sober for 14 years, and this was not a challenge I was going to face alone.

"We need a break, let's go visit the Cravens this weekend and bring a bottle with us."

Karen was not only like a sister-from-another-mother to me, but my wine drinking buddy, she also knew a thing or two about vintage wines, so could probably price it for us before we got too excited. Although I was finding it hard to suppress one of my new delighted squeals.

A weekend at Karen and John's is always interesting and full of stories, as everything that could ever happen to someone happens to Karen. She is just one of those people that attracts chaos. Or 'Cow-Ass', as Lucia pronounces it. It has been like that since our first stay with the Cravens nearly ten years ago now. During our stay, Ronan, the kids and I had gone to Siena for the day. Her Italian-born mother-in-law was visiting from New Zealand and was also staying with them.

After eating our fill of gelato in Piazza del Campo and getting completely lost in the cobbled streets, we were near the car park when Karen texted me: "Are you still in Siena?"

"Yes, do you need me to get something?"

"Yes. I need you to get to the hospital. And meet me there. Will you, can you?"

"Of course, what's happened?"

"It's Chiara, my bloody mother-in-law. John is off fishing or boar hunting or something and, well... she has me freaked out."

I knew Karen's relationship with her Italian mother-in-law was strained, as everyone's with an Italian mother-in-law seems to be.

"Karen, what have you done? Throttled her with something, attempted to kill her? Why do you need to go to the hospital?"

"Chloe took some medicine that wasn't hers. She thought it was her allergy drops... I have to run. Can you just meet me at the hospital for moral support?"

"Of course, I'll meet you in the waiting room. Or text you when I'm there."

Ronan drove back to Karen's with Luca after leaving me at the entrance of the hospital. It took us a while to find, but I saw Karen's beat-up Fiat in the car park. It was bashed and bruised from going up the side of the mountain, where they chose to live.

Karen texted me, "We're next in line, very quiet here today."

I spotted her just as I got in the door. Her back was to me as she finished her text. I reached her side just as the doctor came out of a side door and called her name.

"I'm here!" I chirped, looking down at a guilty-looking five-year-old Chloe.

"Oh, thanks so much for coming. I'm sorry I'm just a bit freaked out and I just need a sensible head and shoulders to be a second set of ears, other than Chiara. She hasn't half freaked me out."

I had no time to ask questions. I'd leave that to the doctor who we sat in front of, along with a student doctor on the side.

"So what has happened? Your daughter has taken some medicines?" He asked politely in English looking concerned.

"Well yes. She has allergies, and she has these drops for them." Karen placed Chloe's drops on the table. "But she got the bottles confused and helped herself to these instead."

"You know you should keep all medicines out of reach of children?" he said gravely.

"Yes, I know that. These are even out of my reach, but you know Chloe. Well, you might not know Chloe, but Chloe is known in this hospital as being... accident prone. I think you are even thinking of calling a ward after her. Chloe the Climber, I think they know her as?"

The doctor had the bottle in hand. "This is dog medicine?"

"Yes, they are lactation drops. Our dog had puppies, and we had to give her these to stop her lactating. And Chloe thought they were her allergy medicine."

"There is nothing at all poisonous or harmful in these. She will be perfectly fine," the doctor said soothingly, reading the label.

Karen was fighting back tears.

"I'm sorry it's my mother-in-law... She is convinced Chloe won't be able to breastfeed when she is older now."

Perhaps it was the wave of relief and not the ridiculous thing Karen's mother-in-law said that made my stomach tense and my lips press together. I wasn't prepared for something to hit my funny bone so hard on this excursion.

And then I noticed the doctor fighting back similar feelings.

"It's okay, don't worry, mothers-in-law were sent to this Earth to test us. She is wrong, these are harmless. But to ease your worry, sit Chloe up on the bench there and I will examine her and call the poisons unit in Milan," he said in a cheery voice, as Karen apologised profusely for wasting his time. "Before I examine her, can you tell me... does she bite?"

The student doctor blew a raspberry, spluttering, laughing.

"Giorgio, call the poisons unit in Milan," laughed the doctor to the student, "and explain the situation. Chloe will be perfectly fine but I want to ensure Signora Craven is not worried at all."

The student gathered his wits and made the call and explained in his best official doctor voice the situation in Italian. But the response was all too much for us all including Karen.

"They want to know is her nose warm and if she is wagging her tail?"

11

30-YEAR-OLD WINE: $$$?

"If the house has been empty ten years and Mathilda was on her own for probably ten years before that and the brother who made the wine was old at that stage and probably not making wine in the last ten or 20 years of his life... Then I calculate it at being a vintage of at least 30 to 40 years if not older," says Karen making perfect sense to me about something we both have no clue about. We have already polished off two shop-bought bottles of wine over dinner.

We always drink too much when together, but tonight was more than too much as it has been ages since we'd spent time together or even seen each other because of the pandemic travel restrictions.

Karen and John were living the Tuscan dream. Well, what everyone thinks is the Tuscan dream, but can often turn out to be a bit of a 'challenge'. Their stone house was up the side of a hill only accessible along a five-mile white track through a forest.

Their view in one direction was cypress and umbrella pine-clad hills, where the sun saved its best display every evening just for them. In the other direction, you could see the towers of San Gimignano from the top window on a cloudless day if you have good eyesight. They grew vegetables, made their own wine, had a water supply from a nearby stream, which they shared with deer, boars, porcupines, and probably a passing wolf from time to time.

But living the dream has its consequences. The water supply often dried up in summer, so water tankers had to trundle down the track and fill up a large underground container for them. This needed to be rationed, so it was either showers being sacrificed or vegetables. They got around this in their second year when John created a feed-off system from the shower drain to the vegetable patch, reusing the water as an effective irrigation system for the vegetables.

The white track was also used by local hunters to access the forest during the main hunting (caccia) season, which didn't make this family of vegetarians too happy. They were also not thrilled that hunters shot off their bullets so close to their house.

"They mostly shoot wild boar, rabbit, hare, but Italian law allows them to shoot songbirds and migrating birds until March if they want, isn't that unbelievable?" balked Karen when we first came to stay with them. "Game is considered public property so they can trundle onto anyone's property and hunt in most places, and they can shoot 100 meters from any house."

The shooting season starts in September and finishes in February. So lots of enthusiastic blood thirsty hunters are released into the forests surrounding Karen and John just when their kids Chloe and Alfie are starting back at school each year after the summer. They need to leave each morning at 5.30am to meet the school bus in San Gimignano, the perfect time for hunters to catch their unsuspecting prey. After dodging bullets down the white track and taking their lives in their hands when they first moved here, they realised they needed a solution as signs and notices down the track were ignored.

Their solution was to blast heavy metal music all the way down the track from the car at 5.30am to scare off the animals and let the hunters know they were coming. The hunters soon moved on to another part of the forest, except the Sunday hunters when schools were closed. On Sundays, instead of waking up to heavy metal music, the Cravens woke up to shotgun blasts echoing around their house.

It wasn't quite the peaceful existence they initially expected, but after 14 years, they were used to it. They had considered moving closer to a town or somewhere less isolated as the kids grew up but then they weighed up the pros and cons and each of them agreed that they loved where they were, their close-knit family had learned to live the sustainable life and, Sunday morning winter hunters aside, they were living the most idyllic life for their family at that moment. As long as they had good internet thanks to the administration offices of a nearby stone quarry, Karen and John could run their PR business for their hospitality clients around the world. They were the unusual English family up the hill, and they liked it that way.

A Rosie Life In Italy 2

After our dinner of risotto, salads and roast vegetables from the garden, the lads have retired to the lounge to watch a soccer or rugby match. They know when to leave us to it, especially after we polished off a second bottle of wine. It is time for us to try the vintage wine we found in the shed that could potentially fund our lintels.

"The bottles were lying on their side so that keeps the cork moist and prevents oxidation – I learned this somewhere at some point in my life," says Karen, looking at the green dusty bottle I have brought with me.

"And perhaps the blanket of cobwebs festooning the shed regulated the temperature somewhat?" My wine-infused logic was matching hers. "Let's do it, are you on?"

"I think this is an event that deserves our good Christmas goblet glasses," she says, fetching her only two remaining glasses with stems rather than the tumblers we had been drinking out of.

We slowly screw the corkscrew into the neck of the bottle. The cork comes out easily, too easily, in two parts, in fact.

"Oh, this isn't looking good. The bottom part of the cork is not just moist but soaked and some cork stuck to the inside of the neck of the bottle," I say, feeling less optimistic, but I persevere none the less.

"Shall we decant it?" asks Karen, undeterred by the vision of the cork clumps now lying on the table. It is nice of her to give it so much credit.

"I think we will skip the decanting and just go straight for the jugular," I answer, pouring the liquid into the awaiting goblets.

As a wedding planner, I've been through a fair few wine tastings in Italy, so I try to recall what to look for.

First the colour. It is a red... well, sort of red, a transparent red with a hint of orange, let's say, but not cloudy, more of an orange haze. But there are no 'bits' or lumps or creatures swimming in it which qualifies it to move on to the next stage.

Swish it around and look at the 'legs' to judge the strength of alcohol.

There is a consistent, translucent film from the swish level, no legs as such. It would be better described as just one big flabby-thighed leg. Perhaps this means it is so strong in alcohol that it would have killed anything that entered the petri dish of the wine bottle.

We swish it around again and stick our noses in the glasses. No vinegar smell but a surprisingly sweet perfume like a port or sherry.

"Perhaps it's a Vin Santo or a grappa!" Karen says as we both got a little more optimistic.

"I can smell a hint of walnuts," says Karen, sticking her nose deeper under the rim. "No, hang on... I think it's more like... old socks."

Of course, this gave us enough to laugh about for a few minutes and enough time for me to realise this would more than likely poison us rather than be of a sellable vintage to fund our lintels. We need to move on to the next stage. The next stage being the actual tasting.

A Rosie Life In Italy 2

I am beginning to lose courage. "I don't know, with the cork so soggy, that can't be a good sign. We might poison ourselves."

"What do you mean we?" guffaws Karen. "It's your wine. You are going to test it first and then I'll follow. Someone needs to stay conscious to drive to the hospital."

The kids and the lads had heard our hysterics in the kitchen and had gathered to see what we were at. The goblet was passed around for everyone to have a sniff. "Sweet", "nutty", "cherries" "dust" and "Definitely socks" were the aromas observed in our 20 to 50-year-old vintage. My courage was waning big time.

But after a few false starts with several back outs after the count of three, I take a big enough sip. Silence falls on the room as I stand still with the slush in my mouth.

It's sweet, but too watery for Vin Santo. I search for the walnuts but, as it traverses my palate and quickly heads down the back of my throat, the predominant taste is 'splash of wet dog shaking itself dry after being in a duck pond'. Along with a good dollop of mustiness and there it is, the reference Karen had found. Old socks.

"It's really nice. Give it a go," I say to Karen. I didn't realise I was so good at acting. She takes a huge mouthful, her eyes widening, and we both race each other to the kitchen sink, coughing and spluttering.

The goblets are passed again, and everyone takes a sacrificial sip in memory of Paolo the great wine maker of The Workhouse.

12

LARGE JAR OF HONEY FROM A BEE KEEPER: €10

We can see the outline of John outside at the shed dragging out a bag big enough to hold a dead body.

"Ronan, Ronan," he's hush-shouting at our window, not knowing that we are watching him from the darkness.

"Do you think he has killed a hunter?" Ronan says with no concern whatsoever, like when he saw it was unexpectedly snowing early one morning and casually asked me if it was nuclear fallout. He steps too close to the window and John spots him.

John continues talking in his loud hushed voice that seems to be more amplified than his normal voice, "I forgot to mention to you last night that I need your help with something this morning. Actually now, in a hurry. We've no time to lose. Can you come quick?"

I check the clock and, in the darkness, I can see the glowing figures telling me it is 5.40am. A mouse scurrying around the terracotta-tiled floor had awoken me and I, for some reason, even though mice don't bother me, automatically woke Ronan to listen to the scurrying and help me figure out if there was one mouse or two. That's when we heard the shed door creak open and went to the window to see who or what was out there.

We arrive downstairs to the smell of freshly brewed coffee. My head is throbbing from the amount of wine Karen and I gulped like water at a desert oasis the evening before. Thankfully, we stopped once we had sampled the musty wine and had gone to bed relatively early.

As soon as Ronan has his double espresso, John comes into the kitchen.

"Are you ready?" he says while grabbing a few cloths and a first aid kit.

"It depends... what should I be ready for?"

"I need you to come and help me move something." John seems a little apprehensive and is not offering an explanation. He is often a man of few words.

"What are we moving?" Ronan asks John, but he is already halfway down the drive and putting the back seats of his hatchback down flat and the body bag in the back.

"Honestly, do you think he wants you to help bury someone in the woods?"

We stand watching him from the door.

"I don't know, but hey, I'll soon find out. If he packs two shovels, then I will be worried," Ronan says with a hint of laughter and curiosity.

John returns from the shed carrying two shovels.

"This isn't looking good." Ronan gulps down the last of his coffee before kissing my anxious forehead goodbye.

"Perhaps John has lost his marbles. Should I go wake up Karen and follow you?" Ronan has already taken his place in the passenger seat of John's car with the dodgy clutch. With revs worthy of a starting line in a stock car race, the car slowly weaves its way further down the white track. I know where it leads... well, where a portion of it leads, and I know I can see it from the top of the hill beside the house. Out of curiosity more than concern, I take a jog, well, a walk-joggy thing, across the field and up to the crest of the hill.

In the valley below, I can see where the car has stopped beside a copse. I can just about make out the two guys at the rear of the car, but the open hatchback is keeping me from fully seeing what they are doing. Squinting helps a little. I can just about make out that they have the body bag open and are putting on... hazmat suits? Has John some sort of COVID leper colony camping in the woods he needs to visit? Now they have the shovels in their hands. They walk purposefully into the wood and out of sight.

I stop watching them, completely distracted by the bigger drama unfolding in front of me; the Tuscan sunrise. Golden yellow beams shoot out in every direction as the white sun lifts her head from her pillow of umbrella pines and oaks across the mauve and navy undulating hills.

The surrounding wisps of cloud above her can't decide what to wear today. Pink? Purple? Gold? And after some hesitation, they decide today is not for them and they disappear into the wrap of blue. The blanket of stretched out white candy-floss covering the valley below rises to meet its maker but, unlike the clouds, it decides to hang around a while to give the mattress of wildflowers some refreshment before they face the heat of the day.

The lads have returned, backing out of the woods, carrying a crate. There is already a similar crate in the back of the car. I must have missed that while my eyes were being dazzled by the glory of the day starting in front of me. There is definitely nothing like a Tuscan sunrise, and I can now completely understand why the Cravens didn't want to leave here. You can't better paradise.

The car revs in the valley below as John does a three-point turn, sending me scooting back down the hill to see what was in the coffins they were moving. They were an odd shape for humans unless they had squashed them in, but why were they bringing them up to the house and not burying them? Why was I even debating this in my head logically? I obviously hadn't had enough tea. I needed another cup.

Two deer, a mother and dappled Bambi, about ten meters away bound across my path, while to the other side I see the long ears of a hare before his wide-eyed expression paused for a moment from chewing some clover, startled at my invasion of his breakfast buffet.

The car is coming around the last bend. I stand waiting on the track for them to pull into the drive but they just motor past. I can just about make out Ronan's face, which is as startled as the hare's I had just seen. He gives me a 'I don't know what is happening' shrug as they drive slowly by. A small swarm of bees are circling his head inside the closed car, thankfully he's wearing a bee suit helmet.

Whereas John is not. He's wearing a cap, a snorkelling mask and a dinosaur pillowcase over his head with the space under his goggles cut out. He doesn't see me as he is too focused on the place they are going further up the track. As the car disappears around the corner, I return to the house, baffled.

"Just in time, the kettle has just boiled." Karen is up and at her perky morning best. "Where are the lads?"

"Well, I thought the mafia had recruited them but they just passed by with a car loads of bees."

"'B', standing for? Bitches, Bastards?" asks Karen, stirring her coffee.

"No bees, as in the buzzy kind."

"Oh, the bees! The hives, of course! I planted a load of lavender in the top field two years ago so wanted to move the hives up there. They'll get the early morning sun up there and afternoon shade. The place they are in has become very shaded. I couldn't help move them 'cause I am allergic and we only have one suit. What was John wearing?"

"A dinosaur pillow case?"

"I used that to clean windows yesterday. Oh well. Get your tea and let's get out and enjoy the garden before it gets too warm and the horseflies come out." She heads out the screen door. "Can't wait to taste the lavender-flavoured honey we are going to get later in the year now."

The lads are back within the hour.

"What's the score?" shouts Karen, smiling at John walking up from the car, de-pillowcased.

"4-1 to me."

"Is there a match on this early?" I ask, confused.

"Nooo," says Karen, "we are talking about bee stings. The last time we moved hives, the score was 10-5, and that is when I discovered I was somewhat allergic. But the hospitals here are great. Come on, let's have breakfast."

As we tuck into our home-laid scrambled egg and fried up leftovers from the night before, the conversation revolves around the bees.

"Why did you need shovels and to do it at such a suspicious hour? I really thought you were burying a body."

"I'd covered the entrance to the hives yesterday evening, just before you guys had arrived. Early morning is the best time to move them so when the sun rises they can go out and forage and reorientate themselves. It will take them a few days but they should be fine."

"And the shovels?"

"Oh, I needed the shovels to lever the hives up. They've been in that area for a long time, so I thought they might be stuck. But it turned out they lifted up quite easily. Didn't they Ronan?" John says with two bee sting swellings on his face.

"They were amazing to watch once the hives were in place and we opened up the entrance," says Ronan, munching on his toast. "They came out of the hive and turned to look back at the hive entrance, then they flew in small figure eights in the front of the hive." He's making the shape in the air in case I have forgotten what an '8' looks like.

"That's to gather information about landmarks and the sun's direction," chips in John helping himself to seconds.

"The figure of eights get wider and more far-reaching, then, as if they have all the information they need, they zip off across the hills."

I just know what Ronan is going to say next. "We should get bees."

And there it is.

Later, when we are home, I text Karen: "I hope you are enjoying the vintage wine I left you."

She quickly replies; "John spotted large clumps of matter circling in the bottle, so your vintage wine is now cleaning our vintage drains."

I'll keep the other nine bottles safe in case we ever need drain cleaner. The bottles of wine may not pay for the lintels, but it will save us a few euro on drain cleaner.

13

VET VISIT: €10

My Italian identical twins are called Moonface and Spooky. I only intended to take one, but fell in love with the two 'gemini' twins and took them both. Black cats are seen as bad luck in Italy whereas in Ireland they are considered good luck, well it depends if they cross your path from left to right or right to left, and I can't remember which was the unlucky one, but whatever it was, these were adorable.

We know the difference because Spooky had to have her tail amputated when she was little after going into the neighbour's garden to make friends with the dog. It turned out the dog wasn't so friendly.

The day it happened I was sitting on the terrace. The twins were about six months old and I'd just heard what sounded like a cat fight and the dog next door barking. Instinct told me what was happening. I ran to the fence, scanning the neighbour's garden and spotted Spooky at the top of the olive tree.

I called out to Giorgia, our next door neighbour. Giorgia is about 85 and has more energy than a 20-year-old. From our terrace I often see her short, still jet-black hair bobbing along as she trots down her drive to get something from the postman. I've seen her already working in her garden at 7am when I take my first cup of tea out to the terrace and still there at 1pm working at the same speed when it's getting too hot for me to be outside. If she had a motto it would be; 'Who needs a gym when you have a garden'.

I know she has one son at least and one grandchild who is about eight. When they are all together for Sunday lunch you would swear there are about twenty people in there. They all talk at the same time, and loudly. It sounds like they are having a massive row. Maybe they are, but they all smother each other in kisses and hugs when leaving.

After calling her from my side of the fence several times, while her dog went crazy at the bottom of the tree, Giorgia came trotting out. I suddenly remembered how to say in Italian "My cat is in the tree" except I got the word for tree 'albero' mixed up with the word 'albergo' which means hotel. I was pointing at the tree telling her "my cat is in the hotel".

Ronan heard the racket I was making, saw Spooky in the tree and made his way around to Giorgia's front gate. Giorgia was on the case; she locked her barking German shepherd into her pen and returned with a really long stick that she used for whacking olives out of trees.

But instead of whacking olives out of tree, she was whacking our cat out of the tree. I was shouting "Stop, wait, she will come down when it is quiet." Again, surprised at the amount of Italian that flooded my mouth. If I wasn't so stressed I would have congratulated myself.

Ronan was in the garden and looking for something to stand on.

No amount of me shouting at Giorgia to 'stop, the cat will come down in her own time' ceased her determination to poke and whack poor Spooky out of the top of the olive tree, where she was hanging on for dear life.

Ronan found a ladder and prised Spooky away from the branch. Her claws transferred from the branch to skidding down Ronan's bare back, before she ran for the fence and made her way in wide-eyed shock back to our garden where she plonked down under the shade of a tree.

I could see her little body rising and sinking at speed as her heart pumped fast. But she had got here, so she was alright. She just needed to recover from the shock. Her sister went over and gave her a sniff. She sniffed back.

I watched from a distance. She needed time to recover before more human interaction. I went to get the cat box so that we could bring her inside and keep her under observation for a few hours. When I returned to the spot, she was gone.

"She has probably gone into the shed to recover. Or into the house and is on one of the beds."

I kept an eye out for her, but after an hour we started a search party. It was soon going to be dark. We searched all her favourite hangout spots and could not find her anywhere. We shook the cat food box, sent the dogs on a finding mission down to the woods but she was nowhere to be seen.

That's when I started to worry. She had never been out all night; the cats were still young and we kept a close eye on them when we did let them outside. They were always in sight. Except for that one moment when she had found the hole under the fence.

Ronan and I took turns staying up on the terrace, calling her every now and then until 3am. I knew cats went off to die. Perhaps she had internal injuries we did not know about. The thought of her out there by herself hungry, scared and injured made it impossible to sleep. Why did I get more bloody pets? Life was just getting to be a comfortable stress-free normality.

At 5.30 the sun started to rise. It was Festa della Mamma; Mother's Day, in Italy. It's not a day we celebrate but if we did, the only gift I wanted was to find my cat.

We don't celebrate it as Mother's Day as we are Irish and Mothering Sunday falls earlier in the year in Ireland–the second Sunday of Lent, which usually happens early in March. It's often the same time as my birthday, so we don't celebrate Mothering Sunday either as I've already been 'celebrated' for my birthday.

I don't know why the Italians celebrate Mother's Day as they always show love to their mothers. Well, I do know why they celebrate it. A priest, Don Otello Migliosi from Assisi, introduced the idea to Italy in 1957. He copied the American format of having Mother's Day on the second Sunday of May, rather than the old Christian way of having it on the second Sunday during Lent.

It was generous of him to use the American model rather than the Christian. I mean it's a bit unfair that Christians chose to have Mother's Day during a period where Christians are supposed to be fasting and living frugally, it gives too many excuses. "I was going to buy you chocolates but, you know, it's Lent...I was going to take you out for dinner but didn't want to blacken your soul with so much enjoyment during Lent."

Back to the cat. As the sun rose, I had an idea of where Spooky could be. The mouth of a big concrete drainpipe was near where she was resting under the tree. We had looked and shone our phone torches down it, but couldn't see her. We do not know where the drain goes to, perhaps to feed the well. I hoped she hadn't slunk into it and fallen down the well. There is a children's rhyme about that isn't there? The pussy in the well?

I climbed down the mouth of the concrete pipe and called the cat. But there was no response. I shone the torch light from my phone into the drain... it wasn't strong enough to see into the matte blackness so I put the idea I got earlier into play. A flash would be stronger. I took three photos into the darkness and examined them. Nothing on the first, but on the second there was a glimmer of what could be cats' eyes. I left food and water at the mouth of the drain and her cat box open.

After hours, the food and water hadn't been touched. Ronan tried coaxing her out too. He saw her; she was coming to the mouth of the pipe, but then spotted him and backed in.

"We need to get her out of there. She's in pain and it is scaring her," I said, tracing the invisible under-terrace pipe to a small drain cover over the other side of the terrace beside the grass. I lifted the drain cover and saw the tip of her tail.

"Okay, Ronan, get the cat box ready. I am going to pour water down this end that will make her run out your end... I think..."

My plan worked... sort of... the cat shot out of the open end, not liking the feel of water. Ronan caught her and there was a battle for a second but he wrestled her into the box and had cat scratches on his torso to match the ones he got on his back the day before.

"Did you not learn to wear a t-shirt on cat rescuing missions after yesterday?"

"You didn't give me much time to think about it."

We both sat, relieved. We had her, and we could now look after her and take her to the vet.

"Her tail is broken," said Moira, our mini-vet who makes my 5'2" self feel like a giant.

Spooky had the most beautiful tail but instead of her holding it above her head like a constant question mark, it now trailed after her like a forgotten sock sticking out of a trouser leg.

"You can leave her with it just dragging after her or we can amputate it. It is better to amputate it as it can get caught in things as she no longer has feeling in it. But first we will X-ray her to ensure there are no other injuries."

After the x-ray, Moira delivered the news.

"There is a fracture in one of her vertebrae. I have given her a shot for the pain and I will give you painkillers to give to her each morning. You can give them to her in the evening too if you feel she needs them. We will have to wait until that heals before we amputate her tail. Is there somewhere you can keep her quiet for about two weeks?"

I can't help but wonder if it was a dog or Giorgia whacking the cat that caused the injury.

We kept Spooky in the small bathroom we don't use. We let her sister visit, but Moonface hissed vilely at her hurt twin. It's as if she doesn't recognise her or thinks she's too injured to care about any longer; cut the bonding cord and move on, it's my turn to be the alpha cat now.

Looney, our Bichon Frise, or Florence Nightingale as she should have been called, was delighted to see her home. She sniffed her, licked her ears and wanted to play. Spooky appreciated the attention, but didn't want to be disturbed for a few days.

Each day she improved. By day ten, she was ready for her checkup. Her back had healed well, but we would give her another month or two to get over the trauma before she had the tail surgery. We reintroduced her to the main household, and she seemed unbothered by her dragging tail. I thought about asking if we can keep the tail. It was so pretty. Like the way people keep rabbits' feet for key chains. Ronan looked at me as if I had ten heads. "It's a bit long for a key chain."

"Well, maybe I can sew it onto my old winter coat as a fur collar, spruce it up a bit, I mean it's not like I am going to able to afford new clothes for the next few years the way things are going. Maybe I'll start a new trend and make loads of money from being an influencer."

"You wouldn't surprise me, stranger things have happened in our lives."

Little did we know things were going to get a whole lot stranger.

14

WAR MEDAL 1941 ON EBAY: €52

"WTF?! Have we just bought a house that was a Nazi headquarters?"

This is my response to Luca showing me the book he has found on Paolo's bookshelf as paint splattered down from the ceiling I was trying to cover with some crap paint, that seemed to be made from chalk dust and water. The book is an A5 sized stapled paperback with a red, black and white cover with a large swastika dominating the centre.

"Probably not. They would have had to tell us, wouldn't they?" Luca says, handing me the book after I'd given my hand a quick wipe on my trousers.

"I don't know, but remind me to buy a lot of sage sticks before we move in."

'Un Po' Di Tedesco' is the title which translates to 'A Little German'. It's a 60 page yellowing guide to learning German from Italian, published in 1941. Paolo has signed his fancy Miss-Piggy-style signature on the opening title page.

He has marked some words inside–fratello, genitori, madre, sorella, padre–words he may have felt would be important if discussing precious photos in a trench shared with Germans perhaps. And measures of days–mese, ieri, sera, oggi, ora–essential to know what was happening.

Paolo has also marked how to say; 'To be late.' He was going to war preparing to be the inevitable stereotypical Italian.

"I really don't have the time to think about whether or not the house was a Nazi headquarters, but this paint is pointless. It's just taking chunks of old paint flakes and spreading them across the ceiling. Tomo has messaged to say the scaffolding will arrive soon and once that goes up, we will have less access to the house. We need to get what we want to keep boxed and stored, or out of the house as quickly as possible. I'll help you with Paolo's room, I don't think I'll be able to sleep until we figure this out."

We go through Paolo's remaining drawers and shelves quicker. It's difficult as every remnant is interesting and a part of the jigsaw that makes the man that made this house.

Replacement parts for an electric razor and an instruction manual tell me he was clean shaven. There is no sign of a comb or brush, so perhaps he was bald. He wore spectacles for reading and distance. Replacement lenses tell me his sight deteriorated.

And then I find the gem of all gems. "Oh my God, a war medal."

"Wow, I'm going to research it," says Luca excitedly.

A Rosie Life In Italy 2

"No, you are not, you're going to pack boxes now and research later," I am trying to be practical, but he knows I am as eager as him to know what Paolo got it for. After a mini stare-down Luca wins. "Okay, you research for ten minutes while I pack."

I decide the best course of action is to pack everything into the grape crates and sort at a later date. And what I mean by later is when the house is finished. I imagine us all in a cozy sitting room with the Christmas lights twinkling, leafing leisurely through the books and oddments and finding the ideal shelf spot for them in the house. Resisting flicking through the 60s car and photography magazines is easy. As is the handbook of all the places in the world and which fish can be caught there. A keen photographer, car enthusiast and a fisherman. I am starting to bond with this guy but trying to resist at the same time, in case he turns out to be a Nazi.

I'm nearly finished clearing the bookshelves when I find a volume of books following the history of an army company. Perhaps his? They are very thick. Typed and self-published by someone and sent to comrades. He hadn't even unwrapped some of them. I wish I could understand Italian better. But no time to waste. I will get back to them. They'll be the first ones I focus on when we are sorting through this box sitting beside the Christmas tree.

"I've found it," says Luca, breaking me from my moment of dreaming of us all being together again in our own home. "It's the Croce al Merito di Guerra, the Italian War Merit Cross. The first were given in 1918, I think... awarded to members of the Italian armed forces for one year of service in combat operations or being wounded in combat."

"Hang on," he says reading on. "The award was updated or a new one created in 1941 and on the reverse it was to have the wording "CROCE AL VALOR MILITARE", the Cross for Military Valour. It hung from the blue-and-white-striped ribbon as before, with a sword emblem for gallantry placed on it. A year later, in 1942, the word "Croce" was dropped. Later in the war, in 1943, the ribbon was changed to blue and the sword device discarded."

Luca inspects the medal. "So this one has the striped ribbon but doesn't have the 'Croce' on it. I think it is a Second World War medal from 1942 awarded under Mussolini, possibly for the campaigns in Africa."

He's back Googling to find more specific information about the 1942 medal while I'm still wincing at the spider carcasses I'm dusting off from a pile of documents on the desk.

I try to stop myself browsing through them, but I can't resist the one that is sitting on top. Even with my weak Italian, I can make out that it is an official declaration of involvement in the war in Africa, signed by Paolo.

"Why would he need a declaration like that?" Luca says, confirming my bad Italian comprehension with his much better Italian.

"Probably for his pension or something."

"Well, that ties in with what they gave the medal to him for," Luca reads on down, "I think he was a prisoner taken captive at El Alamein...this is really interesting; will you turn on the light?"

"We don't have bloody electricity yet, gob-shite."

"Oh yeah, I forgot."

"Let's get Dad and go before it gets too dark, we'll come back again tomorrow."

"So Paolo was possibly a POW in the 40s, a radio technician during the during World War II and deployed in Africa?" Ronan summarises on the way home in the car. "Isn't it bizarre that they came and took the doors and didn't take such important stuff like his war medal and books?" he says, referring to the case of the nine missing doors that nearly led us to backing out of the purchase of the house.

The weekend after we had paid the deposit and signed the agreement to buy the house 'furnished', which means as is and anything in it included, we visited the house and noticed something. All the old antique doors and door frames had been pulled from the wall and were gone. Each member of the family denied it was them. We threatened to pull out. We were serious. And then, miraculously, they were returned the following weekend. Piled in the front room.

Ronan knows that, for me, for both of us, mementos from our grandparents' life experiences, especially from war times, are sacred. Ronan's grandfather was killed in the Dardanelles campaign. The silver sword his young widow was awarded in his honour, with his name engraved, went missing when Ronan was still very young but the family still talks about it. His grandfather's body is buried in the soldiers' graves in Turkey and we intend to visit it some day.

In my childhood home, my grandfather's hand-written war memoir was kept in Nanny's dark wardrobe on the sacred shelf beside the last rites biscuit tin. Now and again Nanny would let me leaf through the treasured manuscript supervised and tell me stories of granddad and of her brother James who died in France during the first mustard gas attacks on the 29th April 1916. He was my granny's guardian, as her mother died from bronchitis when my granny was eight. James went off to war at 25 and she never saw him again. At 14, I promised her I'd visit his grave in France someday. No one had been there, as he had not married and didn't have kids of his own.

It was a promise I had forgotten until we were driving over to Italy a few years ago with the kids. We were travelling through Normandy, France. There were road signs noting places of significant battles. I had booked us into a B&B–in a manor house in Bonningues les Ardres–for the night. It occurred to me to text my cousin in Canada, who had done a lot of family tree research, to ask if she knew where our granny's brother was buried. She sent me the link, and I looked it up on Google Maps.

"It's 30 minutes from here, shall we go?" I asked Ronan. We had started the journey back to Italy from Ireland that morning at 6am, driven across the UK and had already been through two countries. Knowing we had a long day driving the following day, I didn't want to drag him on a side trip, but the whole family was up for it.

Over breakfast the next morning, we explained in our patchy French to the B&B owner that we were going to visit the cemetery.

On checkout she had newspaper articles out for me, about the Irish that were killed in the first gassing in the area on 29th of April 1916. His troop had stayed in the church before the battle, just yards up the road. He had probably walked past the maison we were staying at and admired it, as it was the most beautiful building on the stretch.

Arriving at the cemetery, I didn't know what to expect, but if a graveyard can be beautiful, this was beautiful. A large but quiet space divided up by nationality and battalions of pure white headstones with memorial books in little boxes on the wall near each section.

A beautiful 85-year-old French lady saw us wandering and asked if she could be of help. Izzy chatted to her in schoolbook French, and soon, with her guidance, we found my grand uncle's grave. 'J Carroll. Aged 26'. Looking along the rows, he was the eldest of those whose white gravestones lined up on either side of him. 19, 21, 18.

Hot gulps rose in my throat and I found myself weeping by the grave of a soldier, a great uncle, no one had visited until now. Hot salty tears poured out for the other lads who the French continue to honour so well, even though most were not old enough to have descendants to remember them now. I cried. The old lady rested her comforting hand on my arm and cried too. She told us she walks past his grave every day when visiting her husband's and son's grave on the other side of the cemetery. From now on she will bring flowers for him too.

"Hey, it turns out the Germans put the swastika on everything, so it was just a language learning book sold in shops, not just given to Nazis. If Paolo wanted to learn German, he probably had no other choice," says Luca, from the back seat of the car. He has become a dab hand at research.

As we drive back to Giovanni's, I'm looking at the twinkling lights reflected in the now navy-blue lake. The same lake Paolo probably gazed on with the same love many times. There's a little old French lady remembering James Carroll as she passes his grave each day. He won't be forgotten. There's a little Irish family getting to know Paolo Legume better each day. He won't be forgotten either.

15

SAFETY REPORT: €800

It's early July. I'm working in my orto when I get an urgent call from Tomo. Any call from Tomo is something to celebrate. Sometimes I think it would be easier to get the Queen of England on a call.

"The water company man is at the gate. You need to get down to the house fast, otherwise he might disappear and not return until September."

"But Ronan is out in the car. Where are you?"

"Croatia."

"How in... It doesn't matter, I'll call Lucia."

Panic ensues but thankfully Lucia is in her car and close by, so I run to the gate and within seconds we are driving at breakneck speed to the Workhouse. She understands how rare and precious utility company visits are.

I'm wearing a sundress and no bra, I realise.

"It is good, you will get better service like this," says Lucia when I point out my bralessness. She does nothing for her countrymen's image.

The water man is sitting in his van outside. His reverse lights are on, but I block him with my car. "Buongiorno".

He's grumpy. I try to lighten the mood with my bad Italian, but Lucia is lecturing him at high speed for not telling us he was coming.

"You should notify the customer."

He's not bothered. He sticks on a meter, but doesn't connect the pipe to the other side. That will be for the plumber to do. I tell him what Damo, the plumber, has said–I need to get new water pipes from the road to the house.

"Why?"

"Because the ones we have are old and the plumber said I needed new ones before he can start."

"What makes you so special?"

I don't think I will be getting new water pipes.

"Tomo, we've got the water connected!" I can't text fast enough I am so excited. Back at the house, I tell Ronan what the water guy said about getting new pipes.

"That plumber, Damo, has not got a bogs notion what he is doing."

It's sort of the straw that has broken the camel's back. We have had three meetings with Damo and the third time the 40+ year old man brought his father, also a plumber. His name is Mario. No surprises there. He actually has the same moustache and stature of the video game character. After his dad was there, Damo gave us a completely different rundown of what had to be done. It also transpires that he will do all the work alone and will need the builders' team to prepare everything for him.

Ronan is not happy. "I think he only knows how to work on new builds and has no experience of old houses. He still hasn't given us an accurate quote. It's time to take this into our own hands and call in some others independent of Tomo."

I have to agree. It's late in the day to be changing direction, but I know he is right.

As Tomo is in Croatia, we gather alternatives ourselves. Lucia gives the name of one guy she uses, Mick Kelly gives another and Anto the name of another. Lucia's and Mick Kelly's guys were solo acts like Damo. Lucia's couldn't start until November and Mick's gave us a one page of price estimates with a single line description.

We feel for such a big project we need a crew and something more substantial than five or six lines. Anto's guy, Daniele, owns a company that does plumbing and electrics. He can have a crew start in two weeks and he gives us a 20-page estimate detailing both electrics and plumbing. He knows what he is doing.

We go through it with Lucia and the help of our substitute project manager; Google Translate. The total for electrics, plumbing and heating installed is €23k. It seems like a bargain, so Daniele, aka Danny Boy, gets the contract.

"Okay Tomo, so we have the water connected. Can you call the builders in to start?"

"First, we need the geometra to create a safety file. This needs to be left in the house for inspection should any authority wish to call, such as the police, commune or fire department."

"Why couldn't the geometra have been working on this while we were waiting on the water to be connected?" I say to Tomo.

I'm beginning to think my project manager waits until something is ticked off the to do list before he even looks at the next thing on it.

A few weeks later, after paying €800 for this safety report, a big fat ring binder full of safety measures and inspection pages appears in the house. I have noticed the address is wrong all the way through it, but I'm not saying anything in case it creates another two-week delay.

So, at last, we were at the point of agreeing the contract with the builder. We meet with him and Mick Kelly. I breathe a sigh of relief when he says he would be ready to start later that week.

"Not so fast," says Mick Kelly. "I need to file the permissions needed with the commune."

This costs €60.

"Why couldn't this and the safety report been done while we were waiting on the water to be connected?" No one seems to know the answer. I realise it's not just Tomo, Italians in general don't seem to be big on multi-tasking, preferring to wait until one step is completely complete before doing the next.

I am now texting the architect and builder directly as Tomo is too slow responding to my texts or emails. He is back from Croatia as Lucia spotted him fishing on the lake.

While building work may take time to start, things happen quicker seasonally in Italy than they do in Ireland. The combine harvesters and bailers are at their busiest in the hot days of July, creating the roly-poly bails that remind me of autumn in Ireland. Fruit and vegetables ripen earlier and my vegetable patch is already a profusion of weeds and too many courgettes or zucchini, as they call them in Italy.

Karen did the same thing last year–she planted a full pack of courgette seeds all at the same time and ended up with about 30 plants firing courgettes at her.

She is not one for waste. We realised this when we visited her for lunch during that summer and we had courgette spaghetti, with courgette salad, courgette loaf and cakes with what she told the kids were green sprinkles because the Irish were visiting.

In her pantry I spotted some dodgy looking demijohns.

"You haven't?"

"I have... Making the wine got rid of 3kg of zucchinis, there's also a couple of bananas and sultanas in it too. It might be really good," she said, hopefully. It was never mentioned again, I think it had the same drain cleaner result as my vintage green bottled wine.

"Permissions have been received and the scaffolding company will start soon," Google Translate tells me after me feeding in Anto's text.

That was a Thursday. Ronan drives past every day to check. The following Monday, Ronan swerves into our driveway. "Hop in. They have started, there's lots up already! Come on, I'll show you."

There is dramatic signage about danger all over the front fence of the Workhouse. It looks like Kevin from 'Home Alone' has moved in, and he is warning any potential imposters of the possibilities that could happen should hard hats, steel capped boots and safety harnesses not be worn. The two old guys erecting the scaffolding, which is already looking like Italy's version of the Eiffel Tower, are working shirtless in flip-flops. They obviously haven't read the signs they put up.

The scaffolding was to take a week to go up, but it ran into two weeks. Which to us, driving up every evening to spy from the supermarket carpark across the street, seems like forever. The house is now covered by a metal skeleton that goes beyond the three storeys and up over the roof. I get dizzy looking at it; it makes the house look huge.

I can't imagine that it can go much higher unless they are actually building a copy of the Eiffel Tower, but I now understand why the scaffolding alone costs €5k.

With the scaffolding in place, you would think they would start work on the roof this week, but no one is there the following day.

Lucia and I are sitting on the terrace after a risotto dinner.

A Rosie Life In Italy 2

"Tonight, the 10th of August, all of Italy celebrates 'La Notte di San Lorenzo', The Night of San Lorenzo. It's dedicated to Saint Lorenzo, who was burned to death, and Italians believe it to be the best night to see shooting stars. They are said to be sparks from the bonfire that burned him," explains Lucia.

I sit and search the sky and eventually I see a shooting star, "I wish they'd start the bloody roof soon."

"So you will be starting on Monday?" I ask Anto, the following day, who is with Giovanni in the garden helping him move something from the shed.

"Oh no, it's Ferragosto! In Italy everyone takes a holiday now, in two weeks we start. We must take a holiday first."

Ferragosto on the 15th of August is the big national holiday when most Italians take two to three weeks off work for a vacation. The tradition goes back to 18BC, as a time of rest after months of hard labour in the fields.

Our roof is the first job since lockdown ended for most of the guys. I am tempted to say that they probably should start working again first before they take a holiday from it.

Ronan is in disbelief.

"Now let's not judge," I say when we are back out of earshot, sitting on the terrace watching a swarm of wobbly wasps. "It makes complete sense for them to take two weeks holiday before starting work, after a two-month lockdown, especially if you have the conversation while standing on your head and singing the Macarena."

We had heard the building horror stories from other expats who had followed the Italian villa renovation dream. There were many tales of builders and tradesmen going AWOL for months after being paid and Italian paperwork and bureaucracy delaying progress for large-cobweb-lengths of time. There was also the story of Diane and Bob, who were left without a front door for three months mid-winter. They set up a tent in the hallway to live in. I was prepared for this and had practiced my deep breathing exercises for when the time came.

The time had come.

"The good thing is we now have a date for them to start and we will still get in for Christmas, as long as there are no further delays. Now let's enjoy summer in Italy."

It has been really hot for the last two weeks, too hot to work on the house. We sit back on our lovely terrace at the entrance of our rental house, enjoying the evening sun with the magnificent view of the lake.

Normally when it is this hot, we leave the front door open so the dogs and cats can wander in and out when they need shade or water but this week we have had four or five wasps flying around our sitting room every time we leave the door open. The wasps are definitely less aggressive here. The ones in Ireland fly right at you and persist in annoying you, whereas here they approach you and you swat them away, they realise you are not up for a chat and move along. They are laid back, humming a little tune they want to just share with you.

But the ones that have been visiting recently are weird wasps. They are flying erratically and crashing into things, including us, but not stinging. We search around the eaves and windows to see if there is a hive.

"Perhaps they are young wasps, just after leaving the nest, and still needing time to get used to their wings," Ronan suggests.

We stay in out of the sun most of the day and come five o'clock you'd usually find me on the terrace for the next five hours, but not now because of the wasps. Instead, I take a walk in the garden and soon find where they are coming from.

There's a pear tree just under the terrace. It's heavy with fruit which is falling to the ground. The wasps are eating their way into the pears and devouring them from inside out. But the pears are fermenting in the heat, which explains the erratic flight paths of the wasps... they're drunk.

"Ronan, let's not plant fruit trees near the house."

"What about that persimmon tree that's right outside our backdoor?"

"Ah, but that is winter fruiting. The wasps will be gone by then."

Mosquitos are also out now. So I either smell like the hothouses in the botanic gardens after working up a sweat in the orto or like citronella; the scent of summer in Italy.

The day the holidays end, there is a clatter of vans outside the Workhouse first thing in the morning.

So after a three month wait, the games were about to begin.

16

WATERMELON PER KG: 99 CENT

At our rental I have an orto, to practice growing vegetables for when I will have rows of fabulous raised beds and lush bambooed vegetables, dripping from well looked after plants at our new house.

My practice orto is about six meters long and two meters wide. I look in awe at Giorgia's garden next door. As with a lot of Italian gardens, there is not a flower to be seen but vegetables and fruit trees in perfect rows, not a weed in sight.

My vegetable patch, in comparison, is a hot mess of different plant experiments; watermelons, courgettes, beans, peas, and tomatoes, all fighting for survival in the same pit of dominating weeds.

I think all Italians get up during the night and weed their beds by moonlight, as I never see them doing it during the day.

Giorgia comes over to the fence.

"How is the cat? I am sorry about my Nazi. She doesn't like cats," she says in Italian. Her dog is a German Shepherd and for months we thought they called her Nazi. Lucia reassures us it is Nancy, but we are still not too sure.

She has a plastic shopping bag in her hand and it's half-full of bulging lumps. There are two six-foot fences between us and between the fences is a ditch. She is telling me something I don't understand and waving her hand in the direction of the top of the fence.

She wants to give me the bag of fruit, but the fence is higher than me. Is she expecting me to reach it? I offer to come around the front and she says "no, no" and waves again. I look and see what she is talking about. It's the bamboo. Ancient bamboo about seven feet long, neatly slotted between the holes in the tops of the fence posts.

"Questa?" I ask in Italian.

"Si."

I take the bamboo from its resting spot.

I hold it across the top of the fences for her to take. But instead she hangs the bag of apricots on it, for me to fish back. I retrieve it and the bag sits perfectly on the end of the bamboo until it is safely in our garden.

Fresh apricots from her trees.

Through the rest of the summer, I watch Giovanni and Giorgia exchanging fruit and veg like this several times. I learn that the same bamboo has been a way of sharing food between their houses since Giovanni's mother lived here twenty years ago.

Giovanni is seventy-two. He has twice the energy of Giorgia and about fifty times more energy than me. I am not sure how many properties he has inherited from older relatives but where we are staying seems to be his favourite as he turns up at 7.30am at least three times a week to do something in the grounds. The pandemic was a bit of a blessing in that sense as I could go outside in my knickers without fear of Giovanni flying up the drive in his 40-year-old Fiat. That's his workhorse. He also has a shiny black Audi which always looks new and, like his collared shirt, only comes out on Sundays and special occasions.

He also has a small tractor that should be in a museum and a ride-on lawnmower that requires a special stick, the perfect length to keep some part of it engaged and the machine operational when in use. This too should be in a museum.

Actually, a lot of the stuff Giovanni owns should be in a museum. He throws nothing away and keeps everything in perfect condition and perfectly stored. This sounds good, but he is extreme. Even broken glass from a window is stacked neatly in the corner of his lean-to beside piles of perfectly stacked old window frames and metal poles from dismantled beds, covered in cobwebs.

We knew he had OCD when we had chucked a load of fallen wood from the forest into the woodpile and two days later he had stacked it perfectly in order of shape and size. We must be a real challenge to his mental health with our car that has not been washed since we arrived and our van that we use as a tool shed or, rather, to pile Ronan's vast collection of unlooked-after electrics with their cables wrapped around each other like a bed of snakes and half-rusted blades sticking out from everywhere.

The one thing Giovanni had not updated was his ladder. He still used an ancient handmade one from the olive groves. One day in the late summer, I thought I could hear someone call my name. After a while I went out the front garden thinking perhaps Ronan had gone to the shop and forgotten his phone and zapper to get in the electric gate.

"Can you hear someone calling my name?" I asked Luca who was hanging out some washing, just to be sure I wasn't hearing voices and going completely crazy.

"Yeah, now that you say it. I thought it was a bird."

We followed the distant calling around to the back of the house and, at the end of the far field, I could just about see someone in a tree waving, calling my name. As we got closer, we realised it was Giovanni, waving a handsaw in the air. He was laughing in delight at us finding him. Lying below the half-sawn-off branch dangling from the tree he was sitting on was his broken wooden ladder and his phone that he had dropped. He'd been up there an hour.

Luca fetched our aluminium ladder from the shed and held it precariously next to the eight-foot drop to the stream. Giovanni stood onto the ladder and, with a last cut of his saw which neither Luca nor I were expecting, the thick branch came crashing down, whacking me on the shoulder and knocking me flat to the ground.

The pain seared for a moment as it forced my frozen shoulder into a position it hadn't been in for a year. I heard Giovanni laugh and clap me on the back as I stood up. Shocked and wondering if I was about to cry, I found I could move my arm above my head again for the first time in ages.

The only thing Giorgia and Giovanni don't exchange by the bamboo method are bottles of wine from Giovanni's cellar and watermelons from Giorgia's garden.

Watermelons are rampant in Italy during the summer. They are enormous and carrying them to the cash desk is like an Ironman challenge, but they are the most refreshing thing to munch on in the 36-degree days during July and August. I thought it might be nice to pick one up at the supermarket and have sliced watermelon left out for the work crew on their first week of work.

At the supermarket, Ronan and I do our usual thing, hanging out around fruit and veg aisle trying to figure out what some vegetables are and what we could make with them.

Often, we see a little old couple together in the aisle. The gent picks up the fruit with his plastic gloved hand. Gloves have always been provided in supermarkets for handling and choosing fruit and veg in Italy, it's not just a COVID regulation thing.

Anyway, this old gent would pick up a piece of veg, smell it, inspect it and if it passed the test, it would be placed in the basket by his wife who patiently waited by his side for each verdict. Today he was tapping watermelons. It piqued Ronan's curiosity, "What do you think he is listening out for?"

"A hello perhaps?"

A Rosie Life In Italy 2

"Do you think a hollow sound is good or a dull sound is bad? Or would hollow be bad and dull would mean good?"

"I don't know, just buy a bloody watermelon."

The following day Ronan is at a supermarket in our town which is popular with tourists from the lakeside campsites. There is a big crate of huge watermelons. Ronan being Ronan can't resist. He goes along tapping each watermelon and holding his ear to it, trying to figure out or be given some divine sign as to which would be the best watermelon to buy.

This Dutch guy comes up to him and starts speaking Italian. Ronan doesn't know what he is saying so asks "Can you speak English?"

"Oh yes great, I am sorry for my poor Italian," the tourist says to Ronan, who doesn't speak a word of Italian. "Can you choose one for me?" he says, pointing at the watermelons.

Instead of picking one at random and exiting stage left as quickly as possible, Ronan spent a couple of minutes going from watermelon to watermelon tapping each with his ear close to the crate, giving his newfound expert opinion on why one sounds better than the other in his best Italian speaking English accent.

"This one, choose-a this-a one-a," he says confidently. When he looks up, there is a small crowd watching. The tourist is very grateful, and Ronan nods and backs away.

When he has finished a quick shop and is at the till paying, he looks over and there are still several tourists tapping watermelons and listening for the magical mystery sound. And Ronan, who will be forever now known as The Watermelon Tapper, comes home without what he originally went to the shop for–a watermelon.

Maybe the legend of the Irish watermelon tapper will spread and attract paying guests to our future Bed and Breakfast where we will grow giant watermelons in our garden and serve them to guests for breakfast.

17

LIFELINE: €2500

We spend our days up at the house, reefing out the old bathrooms and getting rid of as much of the unusable stuff left behind as possible.

In the evenings, we work on the plan to move into the house, going through the builders quote with a fine-tooth comb using several translation apps. Izzy had helped buy the house, and we had €100k saved to renovate it. That was before COVID caused our wedding work to be postponed to the following summer.

I always felt the wedding business was a fail-safe business because people will always get married. It's not a trend that will go away, same as births and death. Funerals are a good business too, but weddings are usually happier. But when writing our wedding planning and photography business plan 20 years ago, we seemed to skip the consideration of a worldwide pandemic stalling flights and forbidding more than six people to gather together.

With income stalled until at least the following March, we needed to use these savings to live off too, so our renovation budget has decreased to €80k. Izzy was in the same boat, living off savings until her stalled contract started again.

"What's a bloody Linee Vita?" Ronan's face is gaining perplexed lines by the minute. "They cost €2500 each and we need two of them?"

"I was wondering about that too, so I asked Tomo about it. It's a safety line. They implant the pole into the roof, so should we need any work to be done up there in the future, the guys can access it safely."

"Do you mean the same type of guys who put up hard hat and work boot notices, then put up the scaffolding in flip-flops with their hair blowing in the wind?"

I ignore his sarcasm. "We also need a roof window installed for easy access. It's the law for all new roofs seemingly, so there was no getting around it as much as I tried."

"But two?"

"One for the big roof and one for the small roof."

"Can they not just shimmy across from the big roof safety pole to the small roof? I mean two lifelines is taking away €5k of our lifeline for food for five months."

"Ronan it's the law, there's no getting around it unfortunately... BUT I have asked them to price the two roofs separately because I am thinking, if we do need to replace them completely, we could do the main one now and then do the smaller, lower one next year. The small roof is waterproof and has been there for a hundred years already, so another year or two won't do any harm."

The small roof is above the side of the house, above the spooky attic, the two big bedrooms and the kitchen and sitting room on the ground floor. While the main roof is over the three apartments and the central staircase.

"It's about time we cut back on our groceries anyway," I add. It was something I had been thinking about and, while I was reluctant to admit it, it needed to be said and done. "€250 a week is way over the average in Italy for three people."

"That includes petrol for the car."

"But we haven't been going anywhere for the last six months."

"I know, we've saved lots on petrol."

"But we have spent that saved money going mad on food during lockdown."

"Oh, come on, what else could we do but eat nice food."

"Yes, but that has to stop now. We need to start growing our own and going to markets and living the dolce vita rather than the Lidl lifestyle."

"Whenever you go to a market, you spend a tonne on vegetables and then leave them to rot in the vegetable basket."

"My intentions are good... that kitchen is just so uninspiring to cook in." I sigh, looking towards the tiny space. "One thing I am not scrimping on in the new house is a kitchen. We are buying the kitchen first so it doesn't become a 'someday' dream again, so don't you dare highlight that as a cost to be cut."

The kitchen stays unhighlighted. Things we have highlighted on the quote to be cut are the "Construction site shack, toilet, signs and various equipment as per PSC". This is listed as €1000. On site there is no sign of a Portaloo or shack and I will be damned if I am paying for using the plastic signs that were stored beside our Christmas decorations in Anto's father's attic of the house we are renting.

We had also received the work schedule so we could see how things were moving along to our move-in date. On it is "Removing gutters - one week". Cost for removing gutters in the detailed breakdown is €75.

On his next visit to the house, Ronan is up on the scaffolding and has the gutters pulled off and dumped in the garden below within an hour.

"That saved them one week's labour and us €75. How much are they charging for removing the tiles? Should I start to remove them to speed things up?"

"NO! Ronan, get off the bloody roof. We're paying them to do it. And it only costs €135. Although... removing the complete roof structure is down as €3200, but before you ask, the answer is 'no', you are not doing it. We have enough to be doing inside." I am saying all this while hanging out of the top window as Ronan is standing silhouetted on the scaffolding like a character out of a Marvel comic ready to rip off our roof.

We're good at destroying things. We knock through the kitchen doorway Mick Kelly had hummed and haw-ed about us doing when we asked. The doorway was obviously built as a doorway, but had been bricked up and plastered over at some point. Perhaps it was to exclude the draft from the front door beside it or to give that side of the house more of a feel of an independent apartment. However, Mick Kelly explains a lot of houses have bricked-up windows and doorways to make the building more earthquake proof. We no longer ask. We do and ask later. We pull out the kitchen. I'm expecting to see masses of insects and creepy crawlies, scorpions, perhaps even snakes, but there are none, not even a woodlouse. I feel they are all gathering in one spot, ready to jump on me as soon as I drop my guard.

There are baths, showers, bidets and toilets flying out of windows and piled high in the garden outside. I am saving whatever can possibly be saved; some old bathroom mirrors and shelves. I find an old alarm clock and wind it up. It's been years since I wound a clock. It ticks loudly. I like it. It's nostalgic.

"It makes me a little concerned that they were allowing a week to remove the gutters when it took me less than an hour. At that rate, this job is going to take forever." Ronan heaves another bidet over the balcony and sends it to the ceramic graveyard below.

"Perhaps it's a week to remove the entire roof?" I am trying to be positive, but from reading the plans more thoroughly than Ronan, I know that they have assigned the entire roof removal another two weeks of work after the gutters. And then the realisation hits me.

"They are just biding time! Of course, that was the first job they had scheduled, and they were all away for Ferragosto. That scheduled week is just a fall-back in case they run behind time before they even start."

"That makes sense... well, biding time on the start week wouldn't make sense anywhere else in the world other than Italy in August... Only in Italy," he's using his what-have-we-done voice for the last three words.

The next day, the clock is still ticking, but I can't find it. "Have you seen the clock?"

"I threw it out," Ronan says pointing to the black refuse bags piled high in the corner.

"Why would you do that? I loved that clock. It reminded me of the one my granny used to have beside her bed."

Three days later, the clock is still ticking. It's driving me nuts. I hate the clock.

Ronan can't hear it. He is still nearly deaf in one ear since they blew a bugle in it at a medieval event when we first arrived. It happened the first week we stayed in La Dogana three years ago. Lucia's father, Emanuele, invited us to an open day at a private castle a few towns away.

"They have a medieval display. You will enjoy it," he told us.

The castle owner, a German recluse, had intended to create a beautiful garden inside the fortress's walls, but during the landscaping, they found the remains of a Roman and Etruscan town. This is not uncommon in Italy. For eras the Italians have had a habit of just building on top of things that were there before, rather than beside it or around it. Karen used to do landscaping in Italy, but gave it up as so few projects got beyond the first dig, thanks to some architectural find being uncovered and the entire project being called to a halt for ages.

That's exactly what happened at this castle, however, the finds were quite significant. Instead of building a garden, the owner developed it into a below-ground museum, so you could step down into the Etruscan walls and archaeological finds below.

Anyway, as we were looking around, quite a lot of people arrived and sat in the rows of seats provided.

"Is it a theatre show we sit for?" I asked Emanuele.

"The show is later. First, we have a Mass."

This was a bit of unexpected news for us. We politely took seats at the back so that we could escape if the heat of the sun combined with a long mass got too much for us. People in medieval clothes arrived and a line of them took up standing positions along the wall just behind our seats.

After another 40-minute wait, just as the priest arrived and walked to the garden altar, the guys behind us lifted their five-foot-long trumpets and blew a very loud fanfare welcome. As the back seat row was five feet away from the wall, and the bending of brass had not been applied to medieval trumpets, the mouth of one trumpet was practically resting on Ronan's shoulder.

"Jesus Christ!" roared Ronan as the hairs in his inner ear were instantly flattened forever by the blast. Of course, the words came out of his mouth just as the blast finished and poured into the silence and echoed off the walls. All eyes, including the priest's were on us.

"AMEN," I roared equally loud to amend Ronan's words into a prayer. A Mexican wave of Amen murmurings followed through the crowd.

We snuck away as soon as there was an outpouring of prayer that distracted the crowd's attention away from the Irish evangelists at the back. Ronan's hearing has never since been the same in that ear.

18

SHOWER GEL: €4.55

There were three sofas and five armchairs left in the house. I was going to throw them all out but when I stood back and saw through the dust and tattered fabric, two sofas and two armchairs have good art-deco-style shapes to them.

I Google 'art deco sofas' and it seems one suite, with its curved arms and a deep seat, is a design from the 1930s. Flipping it over during a moment of bravery, I can see the wood frame underneath is in good condition, with large metal springs and hessian.

I feel I might catch something if I sit in it to test out the comfort level.

"Ronan, you look tired. Sit here for a moment." He doesn't need much encouragement to take a break from bathroom destroying. He's covered in dust and cobwebs anyway, so a few more won't matter.

He sits into the seat and looks relaxed.

"Is it comfortable?"

"Yes very. They don't make them like this anymore. Pity it's so wrecked."

"Okay, enough relaxation, back to work." I had got the information I needed to make a decision. They will stay stacked in the big front room and be reupholstered someday. Although the gold corduroy sofa I am not sure about. Being a suite from around the 1970s, it's the newest and has had a sheet over it. But that hasn't stopped the years of dust embedding itself into the foam seating.

Instead of going back to the bathroom, Ronan is on a Goldilocks roll. He plonks himself down in one of the light-brown corduroy armchairs and disappears for a moment behind a cloud of dust.

"These are really comfortable too."

"Oh no, we will get rid of those dust traps. There's nothing special about them. They are cheap 70s foam based. Cheap as chips." I also have a deep hatred of corduroy, especially that shade of diarrhoea brown. It reminds me of Monday morning physics class. The teacher always wore only that shade of corduroy trousers.

He was okay, but I hated physics and hated Monday mornings... it makes me Monday-morning-queasy just looking at them. "No, they have to go. It's these I'm interested in," I say, stroking the curved arm like a long-lost love who I am becoming smitten with again.

"Maybe we can sell them?"

"You couldn't give them away in Ireland, but the Italians would probably try to sell them at the antique market for a thousand. But really, are you going to set up a stall at a market? Can you imagine the paperwork that would require?"

"It might pay for a couple of windows?"

"Well, you can figure out how to sell them but if they are not gone by Christmas they are going to be dumped... It's a pity garage sales aren't a thing here. Italians hang onto everything though."

I am afraid to put anything outside in the garden ready for the dump as I know it would disgust my Italian neighbours, throwing out such 'good' furniture. They love their old stuff, especially big old clunky dark-wood stuff.

I add a staple gun to the shopping list and vow that I'm going to reupholster the curved-arm suite, even though I have never even made a cushion cover. I have a sewing machine bought in Lidl some years back, but the box has never even been opened.

I don't know when I will have time to do it. We have so many other priorities, but it will happen someday, as long as I don't tire of looking at them piled in the front room. I give myself until the end of next summer to complete them. If not done by then, they will be dumped.

As for the diarrhoea trio, they will be expelled as soon as we find out how to get rid of unwanted furniture in Italy, unless Ronan becomes an Italian antique market stall owner. There is a recycling dump, but it's only for residents. Getting rid of large items we don't want as non-residents is another one of the homeowner mysteries we need to learn, but to which no one seems to know the answer.

We stop off at the supermarket on the way home and I notice that one of the local hairdressing salons is open again. They had been closed for months because of the pandemic, and, as I sit and wait for Ronan to come back with the ingredients for dinner, I get a fanciful notion that perhaps I will book an appointment with the hairdresser. Not for anything major, just to put some shape back to the cut and slash jobs Ronan and I did to my head during lockdown.

I haven't been to a hairdresser in over a year and I have never been to one in Italy. I can never explain what I want to hairdressers in my own language, so trying to explain what I don't know how to explain in Italian scares me.

When I go to a hairdresser and they put the cape around me and go off to get some trash magazines, I usually have a full five or ten minutes of staring at myself in a massive mirror. It's then that my hair suddenly looks better than it has looked in ages. It's like when the pain goes away when you get to the dentist. When the hairdresser asks, "So what are we doing for you today then?" I usually give an answer like; "Well, I want it to look like it is now but daily." Or "I want it cut... but longer." It took me years to find a hairdresser in Ireland who could decrypt my coded requests, and that is why going to an Italian hairdresser won't work for me.

So when I get my fanciful idea of going to the hairdresser after working in the house all day, I did what I do in the hairdresser; I flipped down the visor mirror and stared at my hair for a few minutes and twiddled with it to figure out what I wanted.

As I twiddled my hair began to look great. Twisting it around my fingers and releasing, the loose curls were holding. This has never happened before and it would cost a lot to get the same effect at a salon. Whichever way I mould my hair, it stays in place. Amazing! But then I notice how coarse and rough it feels and it looks dull.

I run my fingers over my scalp. It feels gritty. I realise my new secret to long-lasting curls is cement dust. The very fine cement dust that hangs in the air of every room from the endless rubble heaps we clear daily. It's also adding to my grey streaks that I've let take over my hair in the last six months after giving up dye. I have a weird, reverse, ombre hairdo going on.

But I'm loving the long silver hair that is taking over. When not covered in cement dust, it is soft, unlike my previous dried-out, dyed hair.

Grey-haired women under 90 are not a common sight in Italy. Their Mediterranean black hair seems to keep its colour, either that or the hair dye companies make a good profit here. My grey hair attracts attention from Italians. I am not sure if they are admiring eyes or if they are feeling sorry for the poor woman who mustn't be able to afford to go to the hairdresser to get her hair dyed.

The cement dust is not only affecting my hair, I seem to have an allergic reaction to it, or something in the house as the skin on my hands, arms and legs is red in patches. I bought body lotion at the start to stop me getting workers' hands, but it hasn't helped. It's the same brand 'Nivea' that I had in Ireland, so I know it is not the body lotion that is causing the problem.

Back home, as soon as I wash my hair, my moulded curls disappear.

"We need to add shower gel onto next week's shopping list. We are out of it," I say to the lads after my dribble shower, for which I had waited two hours for the water to heat up.

"No we are not, there's shower gel in there," says Luca going in and bringing out the 'Nivea Creme' bottle.

"That's not shower gel that's my body lotion."

"No, it's not Mam. That's shower gel, you see?" Luca points to the words 'bagnoschiuma' in small print I hadn't really taken notice of. The packaging was the same as body lotion back home. I just presumed it was the same thing. So for weeks I had been lathering shower wash creme into my skin after I had finished showering. The rash and redness were gone within days, and I had no more excuses to avoid shovelling cement dust.

19

ROOF: €42K

Things are starting to really move along.

I have emphasised to Tomo and Anto that as soon as they finish the work, I want the scaffolding to be taken down and moved off-site as I have heard stories of people having scaffolding left up around their house until the builder gets his next job. In this way, they avoid having to store it and they only have to move it once. One couple who I chatted to online were waiting six months surrounded by scaffolding with an uncontactable builder.

The scaffolding guys had finished dressing the house up as a skyscraper and hiding it behind a green barrier mesh like a present that will be unwrapped before Christmas. When leaving, one of guys wanted to practice his English on me, "We will see you mid-November to take it down."

A wave of optimism sweeps through me. If this is what they have been told by Anto, then the work could get finished earlier than expected, giving me more time to decorate the place for Christmas.

On Monday morning, the plumbing and electric lads arrive unannounced, and I get a text from Danny Boy to come to the house.

"Where do you want everything?" They ask as we march from room to room. I need to make quick decisions for the use and purpose of each room; where the beds will be placed, where I want sockets and radiators positioned, and how the bathroom should be laid out. Things were speeding up and were now going too fast for me to keep up. "What sort of toilet, basin? The bath outlet - is it central or to the left or right?"

"I don't know. I haven't bought it yet."

"But which one will you buy?"

"The one that is on sale when I go to buy it? Leave that room, it will be done in the second phase–next year, not this time. I know the layout of the small bathrooms though."

We go into the small bathroom. I point out that the shower will go at the end, toilet beside it and handbasin beside that.

"And the bidet?"

"There won't be a bidet in the small bathrooms."

"No bidet?" a Mario plumber looks horrified. I knew this was going to be a bone of contention with any Italian.

"There is not enough space. We can fit either a shower or a bidet, so I am going for a full body wash rather than a half ass wash."

The previous bathroom design had a bidet awkwardly facing the toilet, but no shower. Instead, it had a half bath, even smaller than the one at Giovanni's. I don't get the idea behind half baths. They are basically a tub for water with a seat to wash your feet in. No relaxing long soaks for Italians after a hard day's work in the olive grove or vineyard.

Bidets I do now appreciate. They have grown on me. So much so I think every home should have one. Although initially, it took me some Googling to figure out how to use them properly by straddling them and facing the faucet rather than sitting on them like a loo. This can be problematic when you are wearing pants but figure-outable.

The roof work crew have also arrived and are working like crazy. We sneak up every evening to see the progress and are always impressed at the speed they are going at. By the end of the first day, they already have about 1000 roof tiles off and stacked them neatly in the top rooms. We still haven't agreed on the extent of how many of the beams need to be replaced, if any, but all the tiles have to be removed for whichever decision is made.

From our spy spot in the supermarket carpark, we can't see how many work crew there are because of the camouflage netting. I asked Anto why the netting is necessary, as it is an extra cost that had not been accounted for, and his answer was "because of the neighbours".

I am not sure if it is to prevent things from falling down on top of the neighbours who are far away or to stop the nosey neighbours from seeing what is being done.

After many mostly unanswered requests, Tomo announces a few days later that the engineer will arrive in the next hour to test the roof beams. Tomo likes to live in the moment. I presumed this meant the engineer would arrive with a vanload of some highly technical equipment for testing the composition and density of the beams, but he arrives empty-handed.

He's an older guy, I'm sure I heard the architect call him 'papa' at one point or perhaps they were discussing pipistrelli (bats) which we have none of thankfully, or everything would probably be paused until the species goes extinct. Protected bats roosting in attics is a common problem in Ireland when renovating. Finding Roman ruins while landscaping in Italy is equally problematic.

Before going into the spooky attic, the engineer takes out his phone. I'm impressed. Even though he is in his 70s, he must have some fancy engineering app. The rest of the lads, including Ronan, venture in. I've more sense. I stay at the door and watch. It's too hot and cobwebby in the spooky attic to risk going in.

It turns out the engineer does not have a fancy beam-me-up app, he's just using the torch app on his phone. He picks up a hammer on the way in and when everyone is in place, including Ronan on the far side, he begins to bash the hell out of the beam. Pieces fly off easily in large chunks.

Very quickly this makes it obvious to me, even without an ounce of a trained eye, that this very large, powdery beam will need to be replaced. But he's not satisfied. Instead, he switches to the claw side of the hammer and continues to bash large chunks out of the beam, shouting "Do you see, do you see?" in Italian over each bang.

Still not satisfied, he goes down further towards Ronan and, with a little effort, wrenches a large section of the beam from a crack in it halfway up and then begins to hammer again, to illustrate that the beam's powdery consistency might cause it to collapse at any moment. Ronan's wide eyes meet mine. This could be the end. The roof could fall in at any minute, and Ronan has no way of getting out past Italy's new version of Thor.

Next, he goes up to the main roof. They have already stripped it of all its wonderful terracotta tiles which are piled in the top floor bedrooms. Ronan doesn't follow this time, he leaves them to it and follows me down the garden to feast on the first ripened grapes of our four-vine vineyard.

After lengthy discussions and note-taking up above, they come down to give us their conclusion. The engineer recommends we pour a concrete floor as the ceiling of the second floor and build a wooden roof framework from there, discarding the beams that are present.

I'm really uncomfortable with this. It is no wider than an Irish or English house. Why the hell do we need more concrete?

A lot of the beams are okay but there are many angles and joints, so replacing just the ones that need replacing could cause problems and it wouldn't cost much more to strip back all the beams rather than just replace the cracked, warped ones and the ones turning to powder.

With that, Anto arrives. Anto reminds me of a little worker ant with big pinchers. He wants to be constantly working, speedy and, when backed into a corner, his pinchers are at the ready.

Anto is always disgusted at himself for being late for a meeting, which means he is always disgusted at himself as he is always at least half an hour late. I think he's late because his grooming takes so long, arriving in perfectly pressed chinos and shirt and immaculately groomed.

On hearing the engineer's conclusion, Anto the Ant becomes very animated. He is not only doing hand movements but his head is jerking forward like he's about to lay an egg.

The engineer is saying the traditional way of having exposed chestnut beams would be best and bellissima, but we are not interested in having bellissima beams. The roof is above bedrooms, which no one will see. It's also not good for my Feng Shui brain and I'm not into dusting high places... or any places for that matter... the beams would be a potential galaxy of spider nests. Just a watertight, insulated roof please with a plasterboard ceiling. I'm saying all this to Tomo, who has graced us with his presence. He translates my long narration to "il bel legno non è necessario".

I try to follow what they are saying and I'm preferring Anto's blurb because he mentioned the word 'economica'. The engineer eventually leaves and Mick Kelly explains he will price the option with Anto. Ronan is confused.

"So you will come back to us with two options?" Ronan asks in broken English, holding up three fingers. Now we are all confused.

A Rosie Life In Italy 2

I start painting the window shutters. There are 33 windows so 66 shutters to do. I've been longing to paint a window shutter since I was about 12. They require sanding down and then washing, an undercoat or two and then painting. Some just fall apart when touched. How to get the wooden slats back into the slots is as big a mystery as how they get the figs into fig rolls.

By the end of the first week, all the tiles have been removed. Anto's guys will cover the open top roof with plastic as it is due to rain over the weekend, and while we wait for the roof options or option.

The building crew have neatly organised the bathroom and kitchen junk we have piled in a mess and, on Monday, they will remove all the current rubbish and rubble to the dump.

The following week we meet with Mick Kelly and Anto the Ant. It's a long meeting. Mick Kelly likes to talk slowly. My stomach is solid from anxiety knots. Insomnia calculations of how much the roof is going to cost over the weekend have tied them into a tight, solid heap.

Mick Kelly is going through the 20-page document he has in front of him, one line at a time. I'm getting hot and bothered, especially as we have to wear face masks. The knots are swirling. I might throw up. By page three I can't take the suspense any longer.

"Mick Kelly, just tell me the final price and we work back from that. If it's too much, we can then look out for things that we can cost cut."

He pauses and is a bit taken aback by my shouting. I didn't realise I was shouting, but after 20 minutes of not knowing and talking nonsense, my anxiety has got the better of me. Even Ronan is shocked. I can see him laughing under his mask.

"Just tell me the bloody price." I ignore their wide-open eyes and raised eyebrows, reach across and take the second copy he has prepared for us and flick to the back page. Roof one will cost €42k, roof two will cost €24k.

"Okay, that's doable. We'll do roof one first and then at a later date revisit and do roof two... Now we can discuss the details." The knots unravel, and with their demise, my fears of buying a home that we can't afford to renovate disappear.

I flick through the quote and find the gutters. Copper. "We'd be happy with terracotta-coloured plastic ones," states Ronan.

Anto and Mick are nearly having babies across the table at the suggestion. "The difference in price is just a few hundred euro. It would be a crime to put plastic on that house," exclaims Anto.

I'm glad he cares so much.

We give in on the gutters.

Mick Kelly explains the roof option. The only roof option offered.

"First, we need to put a ring of iron around the perimeter of the top wall. This is for seismic purposes."

"But we don't get earthquakes around here?"

"It is a requirement by law and the renovation bonus covers it."

A Rosie Life In Italy 2

"Okay to the ring of iron then."

"Then they put terracotta ceiling tiles held in place with concrete beams which are reinforced with iron bars." He draws a diagram.

"Then they put iron mesh grids down and concrete. Like it is another floor in the building."

"Is so much concrete necessary, seriously?"

"Yes, you need the concrete to hold up the walls that are being built."

"What walls?"

"The walls that are to be built across the concrete to hold up the wooden beams. The walls are built with light brick and built like this."

He sketches a labyrinth of walls that would be a hide-and-seek dream to any child.

"They are not like rooms. You can never access inside them." He's such a spoilsport. I was just thinking about the fun we could have at Christmas. "They are just there to hold up the beams and there are wooden beams tying the walls together."

I feel the weight of my future roof pressing down on my head.

"Then we put rock wool insulation down. And then the thick wooden beams go on top of the side walls. They are tied together at the points of the light brick walls. Wood planks are then attached to these. Insulation sheets are laid on them and insulation slabs on that. After that there is a water barrier laid and..."

"Surely there can't be any more layers before you put on the tiles?"

"And then the tiles."

"Will we even need the tiles after all that?" They are still not used to my stupid humour.

"Yes." His eyes crinkle sympathetically. He just thinks I am stupid now.

"Well, at least we'll be safe if an asteroid hits. Nothing will get through that."

The insulation costs a fortune. I have always believed not to scrimp on insulation, but with all those layers, I am not sure if it will make a difference. He has priced two options; a thick one or a doubly thick one. We toss and turn but choose the cheaper.

Anto reluctantly agrees.

"I've thought of a good name for the house, after we have finished calling it the Workhouse," says Ronan as we walk to the car, having finally agreed on the details. "The Bunker."

In the car, I do a quick calculation. "Okay, so with the building work we have agreed on, the plumbing and electrics, windows and kitchen, the total without the small roof comes to 90k. We will get about €30k reimbursement from the 50/50 scheme. If we can break it into two lots of claims, then we would have the money back to pay the last instalment and we would still have money left for tiles, bathroom furniture, paint and incidentals."

Ronan is not a man for details nor for worrying. "That's great news, this is going so well."

I had to agree. Even though my inclination is to think that it's going too smoothly to be true.

I had no idea how expensive incidentals could be in Italy.

20

HOUSE INSURANCE: €350

One of the first things I did after we signed on the dotted line was buy house insurance. It was something my mother always told me to do as soon as you buy a house.

It's important in case your house burns to the ground the day you buy it. Well, that was what my mother led me to believe. She had me paranoid that this could very well happen to any of the houses I had bought. "Have you got your insurance sorted? I hope you aren't lighting any candles?" Would be the first thing she would say on the day we agreed to buy any new house.

She had given up asking us where we were going to hang the Sacred Heart after house two, realising that it and pictures of the Pope and John F Kennedy were all non-runners for interior design plans, even though we were still a completely Irish household.

A Rosie Life In Italy 2

I don't know if she has my granny's last rites box, but she has a metal ammunition box from the First World War that she kept the deeds of the house in when we were growing up.

"It's the best fireproof box available. Nothing is made like that now. It's important to have one of these boxes to keep your deeds in case your house burns down. Don't ever light candles in the house, you'll fall asleep."

"But if your house burns down, why would you need your deeds?" My innocent, pre-teen self would ask.

"To prove the house was yours and get your insurance to rebuild it, of course."

For years I kept an eye out in antique markets for an identical box to prepare for the day that I would own a house and need to prevent my deeds burning up in the inevitable blaze after I had fallen asleep while having a seance-amount of candles burning. It's only when I actually bought a house that I discovered the bank keeps your deeds if you have a mortgage or a solicitor if you own it outright.

"But what if the solicitor's office burns down?" asks my mam when I suggest this option to her. "How do you prove you own the house, then?" This I cannot answer, but I am sure in this digital age there would be some record kept somewhere.

Fire isn't mentioned during my meeting with the insurance person in Italy. It's probably because they build everything with concrete, which I have been told, is because the mafia owns all the cement companies with the comforting explanation that; "It's difficult to find a body encased in cement in a roof or in house foundations."

Also, in most houses, they don't have curtains, carpets or other flammable hanging material. Unattended chip pans feature a lot in warning ads about the dangers of house fires in Ireland. And even though we thought for years that French fries, or chips as we call them in Ireland, were an Italian food, chip pans do not feature in an Italian kitchen. So burning a house down out of vengeance or by chip pan or that blasted candle that haunts my mother, does not seem an easy option here. But our Italian house insurance does cover us for other eventualities that would not be mentioned in Ireland.

"Earthquake damage... How close are your trees to your neighbour's house? You need cover in case they fall on them. Do you have dogs? This insurance will cover you if your dog runs onto the road and causes a car crash. Do you want solar panel damage coverage?" I say yes to the last, even though we don't have a roof to put solar panels on yet.

I also request to be covered in case someone walks onto the property and falls during the building work. Public liability. I had not met the building crew yet, but as soon as I do I realise they would definitely not be dishonest.

I love my builders already even though I haven't met them. I know that's not something you hear people saying very often about their builders in Italy, but that's how I feel. It could change next week, but at the moment I love them.

Every night after the work crew has gone home, we sneak in to see the progress. The first evening, we noticed a pile of broken tiles and old fencing dumped in our garden.

"Oh, it is from another job. We needed to empty the van to bring things to your house. Don't worry, we will remove it when we bring everything from your house. The garden will be like new," said Anto when Ronan asked him about it.

The second visit I notice they have broken a window in the sunroom. The third visit we are glad we went up as they have left the front door wide open and the back door unlocked. "This can't happen," I text Anto. It doesn't again.

Branches from our magnolia trees and persimmon tree have been broken off which makes me cringe, but I still love my builders, which baffles Luca.

"So they've come, broken a window, piled a load of rubble in your garden from some other building job, left the doors open at night, broken branches off the trees, gone on two weeks holiday before they started and you like them for that?"

I could understand why he is puzzled. But I can see progress and that is exciting.

The roof is stripped two weeks ahead of schedule. The thousand tiles for reuse are stacked neatly in the upstairs rooms and in the garden. They also cleaned up the mess we had made after pulling out the four bathrooms, four kitchens, removing the gutters and plaster from the walls, and throwing out the old unsalvageable furniture. The diarrhoea sofa has not yet made the pile. I'm embarrassed someone will think we brought it with us.

The builders neatly divided the metal, the wood, rubble and general rubbish into different neat piles for removal to the dump.

There are certain businesses that don't seem to exist which Italians don't seem to realise they are missing. Window cleaners for one and skip hire the other. There is no such thing. Italians have never experienced the satisfaction of a massive decluttering and filling a skip. But that is because they keep and repair everything. They are not a throwaway society. Second-hand clothes shops are few and far between, they buy quality that lasts.

Unfashionable clunky furniture is prized in Italy. Stuff I wouldn't be able to give away back in Ireland is offered for sale at an online store called Market Place for astronomically high prices. If it's old, it's valuable in Italy no matter how gaudy or broken it is. You can find a bargain at the second-hand shops called Mercato Usato (Uso). These are full of everything from big clunky furniture to glasses, and knives to binoculars. It's where I got my second sewing machine stand. A proper Singer, one made of wrought iron for €60. It will be a washstand in the second bathroom.

Every evening, when we go up to see what has been done after the builders have left, I notice the lads have rinsed their work shirts and left them on the scaffolding to dry. They're a neat little troop. We don't know how many as we still haven't seen them, but we guess about six. But their neatness and speed is not why I love them.

After day five of roof work, Ronan climbed up on the top scaffolding to take a photo of the progress for me as he does every evening. There's no way I am going out on the scaffolding, so his photo skills are good enough for me to follow the progress.

This particular evening, he noticed a bucket carefully secured on its side to the top railing. Inside were two little fat pigeon chicks. The builder lads must have disturbed the nest in the roof, and this was their solution. Mammy pigeon had been back as there was bird poo around the entrance to the bucket.

That night we had a massive rainstorm. Ronan went up first thing in the morning, as it was Sunday, to check on the pigeons and they were in a puddle of water. He emptied the water and stripped an old duster he found in the house of its red feathers and lined the bucket for the pigeons to sit on.

The following day, we met the crew for the first time. Two guys; Roberto and Joseph. Roberto doesn't speak any English. He is tall and gangly with a short beard framing his mouth which is in a constant cartoonishly big smile.

Joseph is the opposite of Roberto. He is short and stocky with smiley eyes.

"Joseph speaks English. He can translate when Tomo is not here," says Anto in Italian with a look at relief on his face as Tomo has become quite difficult to track down. The last sighting of him on social media was biking somewhere in the Alps.

By the Arabic music blasting from the house, I am guessing these guys are not Italian.

"We are from Morocco, but I have here 16 years. Roberto here some ten," explains Joseph.

I think the rest of the crew i.e. Roberto and Anto, think Joseph can speak really good English. In the coming months we realise he can't, but he pretends he can. His English is as basic as my Italian. We fall for it and so has his boss.

He listens to us as speak with a nodding head and then translates what we would like done back to Roberto in Arabic. The results are always wrong.

"As you are from Morocco, I am guessing his name is not Roberto?" I say to Joseph.

"You are right, it is Omar (with an unpronounceable bit on the end)."

I try to say it, but my tongue is tripping me up. They are both chuckling but appreciate my effort.

"You see! That is why he is called Roberto here. Roberto is good." I am not sure if he means that using the name Roberto is fine or if he is trying to sell Roberto's services to me.

Joseph soon has his wallet out and is showing me a photo of his little girl and his lovely wife. He also has a more tattered, faded photo of his mother, who is back in Morocco and he sadly tells me he hasn't seen her in a long time. In his broken English and my broken Italian, we bond over missing our mothers.

"How are the pigeons?" Ronan asks Joseph after Anto has left our short meeting. Joseph doesn't understand the question, so Ronan does a chicken dance and points at the roof. I try to translate but hesitate as I need to be careful not to say tetti rather than tetto... I've been down that road before confusing my bust with the roof.

"Ah, the birds! They are happy. It was you who made their bed?... We were very confused when we arrived this morning.

The nest of red feathers, we were looking in the trees for a parrot."

So that is why I fell in love with my Moroccan builders. If they did such a caring job at building a home for these little creatures, I feel they will do a good job fixing up our nest.

21

FOUR PERSIMMONS: €2.99

I've come to the conclusion that if you name your son Mario in Italy, you are sealing his destiny to be a plumber. We've met four plumbers in the last two months and three of them have been called Mario.

When we met to sign the final contract with Danny Boy's company, he wanted to wait until the roof was finished before his crew started.

"How does the lack of a roof stop you doing the prep and running the cables and piping for the ground and first floor?" I ask.

"We like to come in, get the job done in two or three weeks and be out again."

"This job will need more of a commitment, nearly lifelong commitment I would say. We want the first two floors finished by 30th of October."

"The first two floors, not the ground floor?" he asked in Italian, which I understood without using my translation app.

"I mean the ground floor and the first floor. Not the top floor. I mean the second floor. If you can start immediately, you've got the job." I needed my app for this.

We chose well. I signed the contract on a Friday, and there were six guys working in the house on Monday.

Danny Boy is the manager of the business. He's young and looks like he constantly has a migraine or is hungover. Mario, the chief plumber assigned, is great, so I call him Super Mario. He has about 100 words of English and I still have only about 300 words in Italian, so my new project manager, Google Translate, comes in handy. However, looking back on the texts sent between us on the first day, the possessive tense tends to come in at the wrong time.

Just as I thought life was going to get easier now that the builders, plumbers and electricians were on site, Super Mario sends me an urgent text. My trusty project manager app is on hand to translate:

Super Mario: "I need to meet with the geometra asap, otherwise we can't continue."

Me: "What is the problem?"

Super Mario: "It is a serious problem with the drainage of the sewerage. There is no pit. You only have an old, small hole."

I try not to take offence.

Me: "I think you are looking at my old hole, which is no longer in use? I think it was there before they connected the house to the public system. The house is on the public sewerage (black water) system. They reassured me this several times when I was buying the house."

Super Mario: "Are you sure?"

Me: "Well, that is what I was told. I'm quite sure my old hole is no longer in use."

Super Mario: "Tomorrow we meet at 8.30am with the geometra, as we cannot continue without knowing if your old hole in the rear is still being used."

Again, I try not to be offended.

At 8.30am I arrive. There are four guys standing around, staring into the old hole in the back garden. I have only met Danny Boy, and I don't know which one is Mario.

I walk up beside them and stare into the hole. There is a hose filling it with water. I say 'hi' and introduce myself. I'm not sure if they didn't hear me or are just being polite. They nod at me shyly and say a few things now and then in Italian, which I don't understand.

It's difficult enough for me trying to understand Italian at the best of times, but when everyone is muffled behind face masks, it's impossible. I nod back and hope they can tell by my eyes that I am smiling at them. Danny Boy arrives about five minutes after me. I didn't recognise him as it was the first time I've seen him without a mask and didn't realise he has a beard.

"Hey Rosie!"

"Ahh, she is the owner!" says a stocky guy with a cheerful face, who turns out to be Mario. They all laugh. My anxiety about finding a solution to this problem which could cost thousands makes me forget that none of the guys around staring at my hole know who I am.

Mario has a little English. He explains in a few broken-up words; they thought I was just some random person who walked in off the street as I was not responding to their questions, just smiling and nodding.

"Have you put water down the toilet pipe?" I ask in broken Italian.

"Yes, it arrived here. But there is another pipe out of this pit so they will fill it with water and try to find where that goes," says Mario.

It looks like it is heading towards the lake. This could be costly. Very costly. I'm wondering if I can get my money back on the house if they sold it under false pretences. There is no way we can afford to get a new septic tank system installed. From my experiences in Ireland, I am guessing it will cost 10-15k.

We're all walking around the garden looking for something that might be a cover to an opening of another mysterious hole I might own. Mick Kelly arrives and joins in the search.

Eventually, Mario sees a concrete step between us and the neighbour's fence with what looks like a lid. After much effort, they lift the lid and there it is: water running from a pipe that is facing in the direction of my old hole. There is also a feed in from the neighbour's garden and then, between the two pipes, a larger concrete pipe that runs back up between the two houses on my side and out towards the road. I breathe a sigh of relief; the house is on the mains sewerage.

Mario reassures me that my old hole is just a service point and it is still in perfect shape. I do not need to replace it, it will work perfectly again in the future as old holes were built to last, they are much better than new holes.

As he is here, Mick Kelly and I go up to the top floor to inspect the roof. Or lack of roof. We stare up through the skeleton of beams at the blue sky above and give Omaroberto, as he is now called, a wave.

"They will do a good job. It will be a beautiful roof," reassures Mick Kelly.

It's been a long morning of hole searching and it's after 12, so I tell him I am going to lunch. "Pranzo." I am confident with this word and have used many times during weddings to tell vendors that I'm going for lunch.

Mick Kelly's face reddens a little. "You know you have just invited me to lunch?"

"No, I haven't. I am just telling you I am going to lunch."

"To say you are going to lunch you need to say 'Vado a pranzo,' otherwise you are inviting the person to lunch."

Now I'm the one blushing, as I think back to all the photographers, musicians and priests I have invited on a lunch date at past weddings over the years.

"English it is from now on then."

The next day I need to visit the house at the request of the head plumber to discuss the bathroom furniture.

Outside, I've noticed they have cut the channel from the back of the house for the sewer pipe to go to my hole. I had asked them to be careful of the ancient persimmon fruit tree that stands to the side of where the channel is to be. Sure enough, they haven't cut through the main taproot that is running in their line of work. Instead, Mario explains they will channel under it.

I told you before, I love my builders. I now love my plumbers too, even though they are hacking lumps out of my walls.

It is September and Facebook reminds me that on this day two years ago I had a big surprise Italian-style dinner for my parents' 60th wedding anniversary. My 84-year-old Mam says it was the best day of her life.

They fell in love with Italy during their trip, so much so that they decided they want to move to Italy. Us buying the house makes that all the more possible as there is an apartment with no steps and easy access which would be perfect for them. The pandemic has delayed this dream, unfortunately, but we hope early next year we can still make it possible.

Grape season is in full swing and Giovanni pops by to see the house, so I take him to visit to our 'vineyard'. Some bunches of the dark purple grapes are ready for picking; gorgeous sweet, slightly strawberry flavoured grapes.

"Americano," says Giovanni, telling me the name of the grape. Brought here from the Americas, more of an eating grape than a wine-making grape, which suits us fine.

He has also spotted the persimmon fruit tree growing at the back of the house where our courtyard will be. I tell him I don't like them. He finds this unbelievable and decides I must be using the incorrect Italian words, as there is no way someone couldn't like to eat persimmon fruit. He goes to great lengths to instruct me to put five apples in a pot or bucket, then layer the persimmon fruit on top, cover and leave for five days and then they are delicious.

I'll give it a go to keep him happy. But I'm happy to leave them on the tree. When the leaves fall and the fruit is ripe in early winter, they look like Christmas tree baubles. They'll save me money on Christmas garden decorations.

22

LARGE COOKING POT: €15

It has been extra stormy all week; thunder, lightning and deluges of rain, enough to fill Lake Trasimeno for the year. Not the ideal weather to have while the roof of the house has been removed and the new one is supposed to go on. Joseph and Omaroberto did their best to put a tarp over the house. However, nothing but a solid roof could keep that amount of rain out. Bellies of water form on the tarp and sometimes give way at certain points.

The continuous wet patch on the stairs shows the course of the river that eventually found its place of rest in the ground floor hallway. A miniature prehistoric landscape has developed; terracotta islands with high mountains of rubble surrounded by seas and oceans on the three floors. Together with the walls, which have weird shapes spray painted onto them, mapping where they will be carved out for electrics and pipes, the place looks like a badly kept crack den.

We continue to sneak in every evening after the crew has gone, to see the progress, or in the case of this week, the damage.

Ronan climbs up on the top scaffolding and checks in on the pigeon babies. They are still doing well in their red feathered bucket. They'll soon be big enough to fly the nest. I'm a bit jealous they got to live in the house before me.

Last Sunday evening, Ronan, with the help of a spare scaffolding pole, expertly emptied some of the water bellies on the roof tarp above in case they gave way. It was going well until the scaffolding pole he was using went straight through one of the said bellies, and he was suddenly standing directly under his homemade version of Niagara Falls. While I grabbed a large plastic bucket to catch at least some of the fallout, a saturated Ronan jumped out of the way.

It was like a beautiful synchronised contemporary ballet; me with the bucket, Ronan with the pole and the waterfall backdrop, especially the part when Ronan backed into the makeshift platform the builders had just constructed that day to reach the centre of the room, it wobbled and began to keel over to the side.

I watched in horror at the falling heavy metal poles, as Ronan did an impressive final *Grand Jete* across our own newly formed swan lake on the second floor just in time to save himself. The scaffolding crashed and wedged itself against the wall in a perfect parallelogram.

Thirty-five years ago, I foolishly asked my maths teacher why we had to learn the word 'parallelogram'. Like algebra, I felt I would never use it. He wisely said it would be useful some-

A Rosie Life In Italy 2

day. Now I know what he meant, as it perfectly describes the final shape of the scaffolding when my husband nearly got beheaded in Italy. Thank you Mr Maxwell, although I still have never found the need for algebra, but, I suppose, there is still time.

"Will we just deny we were here today?"

"Good idea."

We emptied the full bucket out the window and snuck back out the way we came in.

To amuse myself indoors at Giovanni's during the torrential downpours that seemed to have taken over September, I collect figs from the multitude of fig trees on the grounds, with a glut of fruit ripe for the picking. Fig trees grow like weeds in Umbria. We have several fig trees at The Workhouse. Two have lodged themselves between the walls and cement ground that surrounds the house.

Figgus Diccus Chutney is being made. It is my first time attempting chutney. My granny used to make tomato chutney every year at home in Dublin. I always hated the annual chutney-making-day and avoided trying to take that day off school as the smell of boiled vinegar filled the house for hours.

Now, the same smell is filling my rental house here in Italy, but instead of hating it, I'm loving the memories it's bringing back. Mam crooning Mario Lanza while chopping cooking apples, and Nanny by the stove, stirring the big pot that only came out for chutney-making and boiling the ham at Christmas. Chutney-making took place in autumn, so the winter wardrobe addition of a square of red flannel pinned to Nanny's vest with a safety pin and a miraculous medal would stick up from the neckline of her cotton dress.

The square of red flannel was her safeguard against getting a bad chest. It didn't always work and her bad chest would ultimately lead to a last rites session and the annual Christmas miracle of Nanny being resurrected, and a party.

She'd have probably been better off switching to wool jumpers and trousers, but she found those clothes too claustrophobic. So, she forever wore the same shaped cotton dresses that Mam had made for her on the old Singer sewing machine. All her dresses were made using a carefully picked apart old dress as a pattern. It had fitted her well once some years back, loose in the right places and easy to put on. When it was threadbare, it became the pattern for the only shape dress she'd wear for as long as I remember.

The red flannel was not her only homemade preventive medical device. She also kept a sizeable chunk of yellow sulphur near her feet under the bottom sheet of her bed. Meant for dogs' water bowls to help keep them cool, the sulphur, according to Nanny, stopped her legs from twitching. But all it did for me was stick into my back when my bed was at the end of her bed for a stint when I was little.

Nanny's chutney concoction of cooking apples and green tomatoes has been replaced with figs. I have become very fond of figs since moving to Italy. They are great with ice cream and the chutney is great with cheese, especially cheddar cheese which is difficult to find in Italy. But any hard Italian cheeses such as Pecorino will do too.

Even though I am taking online classes and trying my best, Italian is a minefield. One letter wrong at the end of a word pronunciation such as an o instead of an 'a' or 'a' instead of an 'e' and you have just gone from ordering something innocent on the menu to discussing porn at the deli counter without even knowing it.

Pecorino is one of those words you definitely want to keep in the masculine form with the final 'o' in Italy. Other words cannot be pronounced in Ronan's way, by just adding an 'o' onto the end of everything, such as the word for fig. Under no circumstances should you ask for pecorina to go with your figo at the deli counter – you've just casually asked to have sex in the doggie-style position to go with your very rude way of referring to female genitalia.

Another example is when ordering French fries or chips as we call them in Ireland. Patatine, is the plural word and trust me when I say that you should keep it in the plural. As patatina, with a final 'a' is a single French fry/potato chip/crisp. It, like so many other slightly mis-pronounced words in Italy, is also a slang word for the female genitalia. I have learnt that it's best to keep it in the plural and always combine with fritte so there is no chance of misunderstandings.

I buy a massive pot like the one Nanny used to have, and leave my chutney bubbling away on the stove. Preservative jars and equipment are for sale everywhere during autumn in Italy. Huge saucepans for making passata on outside fires and all sorts of wooden spoons for testing and tasting. The chutney recipe I use says that it gets better with age, I know ours won't last long enough to find out.

While I am sweating over the hot stove and listening to Luca complaining about the boiling vinegar smell, Anto sends me a text to ask me to keep Ronan away from the scaffolding without supervision, he's too much of a liability as he is not covered by Anto's insurance.

So while I stir, I need to think of a way of distracting my three-year-old husband from the big boys' climbing frame and keep him in the sand pit building castles. I'll get him to focus on the bathroom with me. It needs to be done ASAP and is safely on the ground floor. We need to find a stand for the hand-basin. I don't like the laminated ones in the shops and anyway they cost a fortune.

I leave the pot to bubble and I scroll the internet for inspiration and with the memory of my Mam making Nanny's dresses on the Singer sewing machine; I get an idea for the bathroom.

23

OLD SINGER SEWING MACHINE: €60

The September weather continues to be disastrous. The work on the roof had to stop, but the guys have been busy stripping the tiles from all the bathroom and kitchen walls.

The electricians and plumbers are now working inside and have been busy chiselling deeply into the stone walls. There's about nine or ten men working in the house. The hive of activity makes me smile. However, while we have gotten over our discomfort of the amount of concrete suggested for the roof, the amount of deep chiselling throughout the house is now also concerning. I think plasterboard is a fairly new concept for Italy. The mafia seems to have made the Italians develop a love of concrete, whether they like it or not.

"You must bury water pipes and electrics into the wall in Italy," Super Mario explains.

"What if there is a leak? What if you hit a nail into a pipe?" I ask.

There is no answer to this other than the entire wall and all below it would be 'destroyed'.

With a week to go to the end of September, the downstairs bathroom has been stripped, and the walls chiselled out like they were trying to create a complex underground system for mice and cockroaches to travel freely through. I fought with them to finish preparing this room first so that we can get one bathroom working and we can move in before the deadline, which I keep telling them is the 31st of October.

It's a tiny room. We have two more identical to this on each of the floors above. They have chiselled into the redbrick wall. But this side will be covered in plasterboard.

"Why chisel it out and weaken it when we are covering it with plasterboard?" I text Tomo, but I don't get an answer. So I ask Super Mario, he shrugs, "It's how it is done in Italy."

No one seems to understand my point. Or no one seems to understand the point of the work they have just done. And yet two weeks later they do the same to the two bathrooms above, which will also be covered in plasterboard.

Over the previous months, during all the delays, I have had time to build extensive online mood boards of ideas. I don't have a bathroom aesthetic. Well, I do. I have several, but none of the rest of the family can see my vision when I present the ideas to them. I start presenting them with mediocre normal bathrooms. There are objections. I hate them too.

We go shopping for tiles and fixtures and nothing catches my attention. We need to get things ordered otherwise there will be a lull in the work and we'll potentially lose the plumbers to another job. I arrange a day when Izzy is free for Ronan,

A Rosie Life In Italy 2

Luca and I to go to the bathroom and tile shop. Izzy joins us by video chat.

"We need to buy things, today. There will probably be a delivery time so no more waiting around," I insist.

Buying toilets should be easy. It's not. We eventually settle on one style. The one we choose has a seat that won't be too expensive to replace and is on the more petite size so that it doesn't take up a lot of space in the bathroom.

We buy two shower sets too. One is matte black just because we all like it and one silver which was Luca's choice for his bathroom. Even though his bathroom probably won't be done for another year, I feel we need to make some progress and, judging from their enthusiasm, I doubt if I will get the two lads back to bathroom shop again. Both are rain showers with square heads.

We are all drooling at the thought of having a shower to walk into without a shower curtain sticking to our asses and a mixer we can adjust without the fear of getting scalded or hypothermia. None of us can agree on tiles.

"I'd like to create a spa-like feeling; like you are outdoors in the forest or in a cave under a waterfall feel," I say, trying to explain my vision.

"What? You want moss on the walls and slippy slime on the floor?" says Luca.

"And salmon jumping out of the toilet?" Izzy says, followed by Ronan, "And the possibility of being attacked by a wild animal?"

My family are a snarky bunch with no appreciation of my taste.

Ronan says he's easy, he'll go along with anything... Just nothing any of us are suggesting.

"Get the toilets that hang from the wall. They are the easiest to clean around. Especially if you are running a bed and breakfast. And get this brand of flush," texts Lucia after I have told her why we are not at home when she called. "It hides in the wall."

I grew up with a sticky ball cock. Anyone who has lived in a house with a sticky ball cock understands how important it is to be able to lift off the ceramic cover of a toilet cistern and adjust the screw when your ballcock gets stuck. I've known how to fix a broken flush since I was toilet trained. Burying a cistern in the wall and not being able to manhandle my ballcocks should they stick makes me uneasy.

"What do you do if your ballcock gets stuck?" I ask Lucia over dinner later that day. She has 40 bathrooms in her agriturismo which she is gradually updating so knows a lot about plumbing for a 30-year-old non-plumber.

"They don't. They are the best make in the world," says Lucia, a hater of Italians but as proud as hell to be one when it comes to toilet fittings.

I realise it is Lucia I should have gone toilet shopping with, not the lads. Two weeks later I am back in the shop with Lucia and changing the order. None of the family will notice. It costs me €30 to make the change. And will take a new 20 days to deliver. While with Lucia, we both agree on some tiles, they are rectangular white matte tiles each about a foot long.

"They can go on the walls and I'll find something to complement them to go on the floor. No one can object to white tiles and if they do find them offensive, they have another four bathrooms to choose to use."

They'll take 20 days too. I wonder what this place keeps in their big warehouse if it's not a product available for sale.

Thinking back to my Mam and her Singer sewing machine gave me an idea for the wash-hand basin stand. I drag Ronan to a mercato usato and find a proper wrought-iron Singer sewing machine stand for €60. It will be a washstand in the second bathroom.

As soon as we bought the 'furniture' for the bathrooms in the new house, we slowly started to see faults in our current situation, which we had happily tolerated to that point. We all begin to vocalise how much we hate the half bath, which is basically a shower tray with sides without a shower.

We installed a makeshift shower and shower curtain when we moved in. It did the job. But now that we are designing our new bathrooms based on a wish list of what we didn't want from previous house experiences, the anxiety rises. We want it now. Conversations over dinner always evolve back to dreaming about not having to wait four hours for the water boiler to heat between each shower use. And dreams of luxurious rain showers rather than baby's dribble.

The kitchen is another cause of impatience. I am still miffed by the size of the kitchens in houses in Italy. I've said it before, but I still wonder how they have become the master chefs of the world with matchbox-sized kitchens.

We were so blinded by the possibility of moving to Italy the first time we saw the rental, that we didn't notice that there was zero storage space, other than one double cupboard over the sink and zero surface space which we solved by dragging in a pasta making table from one of the many hallways and we have been using stacked grape crates under the table as storage for food and pots.

The kitchen is so small that as soon as two people are in there at any one time, I know something is going to be knocked over and broken. The tiny kitchen has a doorway from the sitting room and another doorway, which took up a full wall, to a hallway leading to a bedroom. A whole end of the already small kitchen was lost space to doorways.

Another wall was taken up with an old, wood-burning range that was once the cooking hub of the kitchen. It was no longer in use, so we installed temporary shelves over it to give us some more storage space.

After six months of struggle, we bought ourselves a new cooker and installed it facing the sitting room door so that when the oven door was open, we could stand in the open doorway, giving us less chance of burning ourselves. Having a kitchen with zero surface space to put used dishes on for washing meant, as soon as you had a meal, and the used dishes and pots were put in the tiny space beside the sink, the kitchen looked like a scene from one of those 'I'm addicted to hoarding' TV shows where you just wonder how anyone lives like that.

The water supply is from the well in the garden, but Giovanni told us it is not drinkable. It had not been tested in years and I'd say the supply pipes are fairly rusty. We have to buy in bottled water, which leads us to producing a cringe-worthy mountain of plastic waste each week. Only now, weeks before we are due to leave the house, I have discovered a lot of towns, including our own local one, have a water refill machine tucked away somewhere, where you can fill your own bottles of clean water.

The joy of being on a public water system again in our new house is a very exciting prospect. However, the water in Italy is hard, even the bottled water leaves a limey residue on glasses if left for any period of time so we have ordered a water softener to be installed which will save us having to replace the dishwasher, kettle and washing machine because of eventual limescale build up.

Speaking of washing machines, the one we have in our rental is in the bathroom with the outlet hose needing to be placed in the bath when in use. If we forgot to put it in the bath, after showering in the half bath, the bathroom hallway and sitting room got flooded with the dirty soapy water from the washing machine.

To help stop potential flooding, I stuck a notice up on the back of the bathroom door to remind us 'Check Your Hose'. I hadn't thought of the wording much until a male friend came out of the bathroom a little embarrassed, wondering if it was something similar to telling women to check their breasts for lumps and what should he be checking for.

The electric supply in our rental didn't allow for several things to be on at once, such as an electric kettle, toaster and washing machine. A limited electric supply is common in most houses in Italy. An electric kettle on at the same time as a fridge triggers the trip switch, a kettle on a gas stove is the only solution. There was no possibility of having a dishwasher or an electric kettle in our rental, but thanks to talks with other expats about how to solve the limited electric appliance issue, we had requested the installation of three-phase electricity.

This request is much to the dismay of the electrician and builder who had obviously grown up with doing one electrical task at a time. Perhaps this is why the Italians don't do multi-tasking.

So our drool-worthy wish list of a big fitted kitchen with surface space, a dishwasher, a proper shower, a washing machine that didn't flood and being able to use several appliances at once is raising our move-in anxiety as we approach the finishing line.

We now all avoid the kitchen in Giovanni's as we hate it so much, so our cooking efforts are getting worse. Spaghetti Bolognese is our go-to dinner nearly every night. Unfortunately, we can't even relieve ourselves from our mundane diet by visiting a restaurant, as lockdown has them closed. This is probably just as well, as we are also resisting showering more often at the thoughts of facing the grim half bath dribble shower and stick-to-your-ass curtain.

Our aim for the Workhouse is to get a comfortable sitting room with a stove, a working bathroom, a kitchen and a washing machine installed. Once these are in, there is no holding us back. Even if the bedrooms are horrendous, we won't wait a day longer.

24

BRASS RAIN SHOWER: €190

While we wait for deliveries, I visit my mood boards. I'm getting a better vision of what I want the first bathroom to be like. There is one bathroom in particular that keeps showing up as a favourite; blue hexagon tile with a white geometric pattern created by lines from each corner meeting a central line. It's the one bathroom that we all agree we like.

The blue tiles are on the floor and stretch up the end wall and onto the ceiling. I mightn't go as far as the ceiling, but they will look cool. On the opposite walls, white matte tiles are quite like the ones I bought already without the family knowing.

After several frustrating hours, I eventually find an Italian company that imports the blue Spanish tiles and I order them. They will take ten days. Weird how they can come faster from Spain than the white tiles can come from a major company's own warehouses based in Italy.

I now know exactly how I want the downstairs bathroom to look, as it's the same as the one in an online house magazine; blue and white with brass fittings.

I haven't been able to find brass fittings in any of the stores we have visited in Italy. Online I find a great brass rain shower, gorgeous brass taps and a brass pop-up sink plug and ornate brass shower drain cover. Getting excited over a plug hole cover is a new experience for me. But they are gorgeous with two fish swimming on them. Brass bass. All are ordered and arrive before the Italian white tiles and toilets.

I'm on a roll, so I search Market Place for a second sewing machine stand as vanity units are ridiculously overpriced. I find one. It's not a Singer sewing machine like the first one I bought, but I like it. The picture shows metal legs, so it looks like it will do the job and is only 20 minutes away; no harm in having a look. With the help of my trusted translation app, I arrange for us to go buy it the following day.

The owner gives us an address and complex directions. We end up outside several villas and turn around in the road several times. "My father will wait on the road. You can follow him."

We are looking for a car, but no, there is a man standing and waving. We turn onto the road he is standing at the corner of and follow him. We're in the car and he's jogging in front.

We pass a distinctive boutique hotel which they live next door to, as it turns out.

"Why didn't she just give us the name of the hotel?"

He doesn't speak a word of English and the woman I had been texting is nowhere to be seen. We go up three flights of marble stairs, passing two other sewing machine tables being used as ornaments. Before I can get to the top floor, the man has already grunted instructions to Ronan to grab one end, and he has grabbed the other and they are heading down the stairs with the heavy table past me.

"Wait, that's not what I want."

"Too late now," says Ronan.

It's nice, but it's all wood. "It really isn't suitable for the bathroom, especially as it's going to be a wet room... and it has woodworm."

"It will be fine," says Ronan, hoisting the heavy machine table around the stairwell.

"Ronan, you are not supposed to be lifting heavy things!"

"I know that is why it will do. I am not carrying it back up."

The sewing machine is plonked beside the car as both Ronan and the old guy catch their breath. Mr Friendly and Very Happy then ushers us into the front room, where he has another vintage sewing machine without a stand ready to show us.

"Very nice, but we don't want the actual sewing machine."

I know he is thinking I have said something incorrectly, so he demonstrates again how it works.

"Even if you did like sewing machines, why does he think we would need a second one?"

"Good point."

We stand politely watching his in-depth demo while I Google how to say "We don't want the machines, just the stand." But the message still isn't getting through. He starts to show us another machine in an adjoining room.

"Bloody hell, how many machines does this guy have? Is it some sort of fetish?"

"Maybe there is a secret underworld of vintage sewing machine collectors in Italy we are now becoming part of?"

"No, grazie!" I say loudly, "Andiamo!" And I push Ronan back towards the front door.

Together we all manoeuvre the clunky but pretty sewing machine stand into the back of our car with great difficulty.

Ronan hands over the €80 without even bargaining. If I had done that, he'd have told me I should have bargained him down to €60 at least. But, as always, Ronan has somehow become this guy's friend on the way down the stairs with no common language between them.

The vintage wooden sewing machine stand was supposed to be a more cost-effective solution to buying a new washbasin unit, which would be three or four times that amount. Instead, we have just gained a large bulky ornament that has cost us half of our new grocery budget... I need to find some practical use for it, so I don't feel so stupid.

On the way home, I search vintage sewing machine upcycling ideas online and find pictures of similar wooden stands being used as washbasin stands, so perhaps it can work. It will have to. I can't afford to be making such costly mistakes.

A Rosie Life In Italy 2

The last week of September, the rains stop. The lads work from dawn until near dark to get the terracotta ceiling slabs in place to get the ceiling 'closed'. These slabs slot between concrete beams that run from wall to wall. By the 25th we can no longer see the sky through the roof.

"The weather forecast for the coming weeks is not good, so tomorrow they will pour concrete on top to seal the roof before the rain is due to start again," texts Mick Kelly.

We are now bypassing Tomo, who has gone very quiet. Thankfully, I haven't paid him anything as he hadn't requested a payment to date. But even about payment, he has not returned my texts or calls, nor anyone else's from the team. I sometimes hear Mick Kelly, Anto or Lucia mentioning to someone that they have spotted him. The last sighting was up a tree with a chainsaw on the other side of town. Trace Tomo is our Italian version of Where's Waldo?

We can't wait for him to come back to the crew. We need to press on without his input, not that it has been much to date. Mick Kelly impresses the time of the arrival of the cement truck and encourages us to come watch from the supermarket carpark... Which is a little embarrassing, as they must know that is where we hang out eating sandwiches watching them work. I'm not sure if I want to watch a million tons of cement being poured on top of my fragile house. I really can't see the attraction, or whether or not it will induce anxiety or boredom.

We arrive at the carpark at the time Mick Kelly has instructed with sandwiches at the ready and we see a cement truck drive by. He finds a turning spot and drives back. Joseph is out on the road in a high-viz jacket, with paddles for directing traffic.

A huge arm lifts out of the lorry and reaches into the air. I hadn't expected this. I hadn't really thought about how the cement was going to get up there. Two guys on the roof guide it down before the creaking and churning noises start. Joseph is watching and not guiding the traffic. He looks fascinated, like a young boy. There are back-ups on both sides of the truck. Omaroberto is shouting at him, snapping him out of his smiling trance and waves both lines of traffic on at the same time.

"Are you sure Joseph is the foreman? It looks like Roberto is giving the orders?" asks Ronan an hour later, as we drive through the second traffic jam Joseph has caused by waving his paddles in the air at the same time.

We're not to go into the house for three days. It's like we've built a nuclear bomb shelter with windows.

While the concrete bunker is drying out, I work on some projects I've taken back to our rented home with me. Some shutters for sanding and painting, the old rusted lamp above the front door and the tarnished door handles. I have tried everything on the handles to clean them, including 'Brasso' I brought back from my last trip to Ireland. I'm starting to think they were once brass coated, and it has long since worn away.

"Try cola," says Ronan, bringing back a flood of cola memories of when Ronan had seen a viral YouTube video of someone using it to clean toilets and dissolving car rust on contact. For three days he went through dozens of bottles of cola, using it for everything, with the only result being sticky messes, a cola smelling toilet and a very full plastic recycling bin. I am sure the video was just a good ploy by the cola manufacturers to get 'curious' people like Ronan to buy cola for purposes other than drinking.

So I try cola. I leave the lamp soaking overnight in a bucket of cola and, sure enough, it loosens and dissolves all the rust. With a grey undercoat and black gloss coat, the lamp looks as good as new with the glass plates cleaned and a new electric fitting for the bulb.

The front door handles just need an hour in cola and then, with a rub of fine wire wool, they are back shining to their former glory. 'A perfect solution for your tarnished knobs and knockers.'

Only three days after the concrete was poured, and the guys are back up, working like crazy on the roof.

"We need to meet tomorrow urgently," texts Anto to me and Mick Kelly.

"Okay, at eight?" I respond, my jaw tightening and biting my lip so hard it hurt. Is this the moment they tell me the house is about to collapse and it will cost the economy of a small country to fix it? We had prepared ourselves to have a few hurdles along the way and were surprised that we got this far without much complication.

"After lunch," they both respond simultaneously. Nothing is more important than lunch in Italy, even if it is a collapsing house. Tomo is no longer even included in the messages. He has well and truly been replaced with an app.

"It's the apex wall on the second floor. We do not understand why they built it the way it is. The ground floor and first floor are thick stone and then this floor is a thin wall, just one layer of stone. It needs to be thicker to be strong enough to hold the roof."

"Can it wait?"

"It's better to do it now."

"Is the house going to collapse?"

"No, not collapse, but it is better to do it now."

"Okay, if it has to be done, then it has to be done. How much will it cost?"

"It depends. But not so much," Anto says wiggling his hand.

Over the weekend, I am thinking about it.

"That wall is going to delay things, isn't it?" I say to Ronan over his Sunday morning coffee on the terrace.

"That's what I'm thinking too. I think we should suggest they wait until the spring to do it. It's on the top floor so if we get them to focus on downstairs and do the small roof and that wall in stage two."

I agree with him. There's no way we'll be in before Christmas with such a big extra job to do.

"I'm also thinking of ways we could keep the cost of the wall down. We haven't had a quote for it yet, but how about we suggest they build it out of the stone left over so we don't have to plaster it?"

"That's a good idea. I can't believe how high the estimate for plastering walls was in the original quote. We will avoid smooth walls," he jokes, but I know he's serious too and hitting a sensitive point for me. I want smooth walls.

"We'll find someone cheaper or a way around it. We will definitely have smooth walls, Ronan."

"Well, I can do them, I have plastered before." Ronan thinks he is bionic and his "I can do it," answer is his solution to every problem. He has done a bit of everything at this stage since we have renovated several houses on next-to-nothing budgets. But this time we had said we would get tradespeople in to do the work, my main reason being is that I want the house finished this century and secondly Ronan is not supposed to be lifting anything heavy or over stretching since his ultrasound diagnosis.

I arrive on Monday to discuss a few other things with Anto and plan to suggest waiting until the spring to do the wall and to leave it unplastered. I can hear his voice upstairs talking to Omaroberto so I follow the voices to where the offending wafer wall is...was. The new wall is already nearly complete, and it is only 11am.

"Oh... that's nice..." is all I can say. It is 'nice', a really good job which Omaroberto is beaming about as Joseph carries him up another bucket of cement and Anto nods approvingly at. It's too late now for me to discuss the wall cost saving ideas, but it's consoling that at least we are flying along with progress and have a very solid house.

I had heard Italian builders can be slow workers but these guys are almost going too fast. Although they are Moroccan, so I don't know if the Italian rule applies.

When they are not chiselling out my walls, the electricians and plumbers are busy building Star Trek's new headquarters in the area under the bathroom extension. It has been a 'nothing' area up until now. Now it is a neat but complex system of levers, pipes, tubes and boilers that NASA would be proud of.

"You should build a wall here, to close it off," advises Anto.

"Okay," I say, "we will." Meaning Ronan and I will get around to it someday. That evening we call back up to the house and the wall has been built. I should have learned from my earlier experience.

The last four weeks must have been the wettest start to autumn in Italian history. Or maybe I am just more conscious of every drop that falls from the sky because of our lack of roof up until now. The bad weather did not seem to affect the work on the roof that much, but it has soaked the inside walls.

We bring Lucia up to have a peak at the destruction progress. Within days of the house being closed to the elements, the walls are already starting to dry out. What were near perfect walls when we bought the place are now streaked with black mould.

It looks awful, like watching someone you love have open heart surgery. Black plastic pipes are sticking out from every orifice like unattended aortas, the walls look like they have been slashed open by a fake surgeon who forgot his glasses and possibly doesn't know anything about anatomy so just keeps cutting deep until he hits the right spot.

"The house feels so sad," I say to Ronan and Lucia. "I can feel the house groaning and asking, 'What have you done to me? I thought you were here to help?' But she's saying it in Italian, so I don't quite know if I am getting the translation right."

"The house has been sedated for the surgery, she's sleeping through it," says Ronan, trying to ease my gutted feeling of the house being gutted.

Lucia isn't thinking of life saving surgery, instead she is thinking of it as cosmetic, and exclaims in an animated way, "She is going to wake up and go 'wow look at my new boobs, look at my new waistline, ooh I have cheekbones again and my wrinkles are gone. I look so young!' She will be so happy, don't worry."

Thinking of it this way does make me feel better, until Lucia says, "but you have moles in your walls."

"Moles in my walls? What the hell, is that a thing in Italy?"

"Yes, they come because of the rain, look I show you." She leads me up the stairs and points at the damp stain on the wall which is distinctly the perfect shape of Ireland.

"They are there?" I'm thinking that's an ironic place for them to take up residence as we don't have moles in Ireland.

"I think when the heat is working, the moles on the wall will go," says Lucia matter-of-factly.

"Ohhh! you mean mould!"

25

DOUBLE GLAZED WINDOW: €200

I love autumn sunrises in Italy. I take my morning cup of tea to the front door and watch it happen over Lake Trasimeno. It gives me a sense of comfort and renewed hope. It is nearly the end of October and the mock deadline is looming, but the guys are working so hard to catch up after the rain that I am not going to enforce the penalty agreed in the contract; €50 per day for everyday past the 31st of October.

One more week to the roof being finished and the weather forecast is dry. I'm still astonished by how many layers and how much work goes into building roofs in Italy.

Tomo texts me and asks if he can use me as a reference for a site project manager's job he is going for. After I pick myself up off the floor from laughing, I sit down with Ronan and we create a long list of basic things that need to be done so that we can move in. The 'To Dos' are listed under the titles: Water. Heat. Food.

Water is the plumbing which is being worked on. There is nothing more we can do to speed this up.

The first thing we need for heat is to get the house watertight. Which means the roof finished and windows in. The roof is being worked on and the windows need to be fixed.

Food means we need a kitchen. I have been watching out for the right kitchen since we bought the house last May. All the local shops I look at online only sell laminated wood kitchens. I want solid wood cabinet doors without laminate, that I can paint a different colour in 20 years' time and know it won't peel if it gets wet or chipped with time. I want the beautiful kitchen I have never had and I know if I don't order it early in the process, the money will be gobbled up on everything else.

I happened to see a notice on a local Facebook group about yoga classes near me, held by an English woman called Ruth at her house up the hill. I've been trying to find a Friday morning yoga class to join since I came to Italy and so I join the following week. There are a few other women in the class. American, Welsh, English and Scottish and now I'm the Irish contingent. I feel a lot of English, Irish, Scottish jokes bubbling up, which I suppress... for now.

The yoga is great but also having people to talk to who have already been through the renovation and building process in Italy is even better. Ruth's house is beautifully finished, and she has the kitchen of my dreams. Before the first yoga session is over I have an appointment made at the kitchen shop she bought it from, 40 minutes' drive away.

We arrive at the small but elegant showroom. Not a laminate or put together yourself unit in sight. What a relief. I see Ruth's kitchen and go straight to it. Holding up our kitchen idea drawing on graph paper with the measurements. And say in my basic Italian pointing at the showroom "black and blue" while holding up my graph paper design, indicating the counter and sink as black and units as blue.

Riccardo, a happy smiley bald chap, brings us into his office and copies my drawing and measurements onto his computer.

With a few adjustments, some Google translations passed back and forth and lots of pointing at illustrations in a folder at the style of cabinet; double, single, drawers, stove options, dishwasher options, we have our kitchen with central island priced and ordered within 90 minutes. It will cost 10k plus vat, including stove, corner hood, oven, dishwasher and black marble counter and splash back. Done.

It will be ready and installed by the beginning of December. Who needs a Tomo?

So the next thing to do is chase getting the windows fixed. I have always found it a bit discomforting that so many houses in Italy and Spain have iron grids or bars on their windows. It's not a thing in Ireland, well not since the time of castles and you needed window bars and hot oil to keep marauding intruders out.

The front doors of houses we've visited here are better than most prisons; three double locks inside and a large sliding bolt that would keep any giant battering ram at bay, at least until you had heated up enough olive oil to pour out the top window.

It made me feel naïve about the security needed in Italy, so during one of our first meetings with Tomo, I brought up the subject.

"I think we should get new shutters for the downstairs doors to make it more secure," I had said to Tomo.

"If security is a concern, then you want bars on the windows."

"Oh God, no, they make a house look like a prison. Are they necessary? Is the crime rate that bad in Italy?"

"Well, if someone wants to get into your house, shutters won't keep them out, but bars would," he laughed.

We priced new aluminium windows, and we priced getting the current, single-glazed windows refurbished and double glazing installed. We liked the old chestnut frames that we had but felt aluminium would be less maintenance. When we got the quotes back, the price difference of over 30k for new aluminium windows versus €6,600 for the refurbishment of the original wood windows makes us decide that we absolutely love the wooden windows and it would be criminal to replace them with aluminium.

We have been asking Tomo about getting work started on the windows since June. They were not something that needed the scaffolding up or the water connected, but still there was no movement towards getting them done.

Then a month ago, out of the blue, I got a text from Tomo; "You need to go to the house and paint the windows now before the carpenter starts work on them."

"Now?"

"Yes, now, it will be a lot faster before the glass man arrives."

It is like some coded message for a spy mission with The Carpenter and The Glass Man as the chief villains. I was in the middle of creating a website and Ronan was mid-axe-swing, chopping wood.

"We need to go now and paint the window frames, before The Carpenter arrives," I tell him, marching towards the car.

"What, now?"

"Yes, now," I feel like I'm having a déjà vu conversation.

"Let's go, we need to buy paint and rollers and brushes."

Two hours later, we arrive at the house kitted out in our painting work clothes and a selection of paint brushes, rollers, drip sheets and pots of paint we have argued over.

We reversed into the driveway of the house and emptied the boot of our painting gear before we noticed something weird. All the windows and French doors were gone.

Here in Italy, windows easily slot on and off hinges. It's handy because, if one breaks, the owner can easily lift it off, take it to be repaired and slot it back on. But someone has come, unhinged all of our windows and taken them away.

"First the doors and now the windows? What is it about this house that makes people feel the need to take hinged objects?"

In dismay, I text Tomo, "the windows are gone. Where have they gone?"

"I do not know. You need to paint them."

"I know that, but they are not here to paint." I stand surrounded by tins of paint looking at the empty voids where windows once were and try to stay calm.

"That is a problem," is the reply I get from Tomo.

We pack up, return home and wait three hours for a follow-up to our mission.

"The Carpenter took the windows. You need to go to the barn."

"What barn and for what?" Again I feel like I am part of some mystery heist led by The Carpenter and The Glass Man, where information is given in stages, on a need-to-know basis.

"To the barn of Lucia... to paint the windows."

"Lucia's barn?"

"Yes, they know each other, and The Carpenter called her to ask if you could use the barn to paint them. It is better this way, trust me."

"But the house has no windows," I exclaim, "Just big gaping holes! There's stuff in there that could be robbed."

"Don't worry, it will be safe," says the same guy who told me I would need bars on my windows to feel secure.

Tomo then disappears back into the ether.

So our job this week is to clean, sand, undercoat and top coat 66 window frames. And then get The Glass Man to collect them to put in new double glazing.

Inside shutters and outside shutters would also need to be painted ... that's 132 items. But they can wait. The windows are the important thing to get done.

With early starts, late nights and constant sanding and painting, we finish the frames within a week. Lucia helps us communicate with The Carpenter via his daughter, who seems to be the admin brains behind his business.

I call Lucia a few days after we had informed them that the windows are ready.

"Are the windows gone yet?"

"No, but relax. The house is not finished yet."

"We don't want to wait until the house is finished. We want the windows in as soon as possible to make it weathertight."

"But they said the glass will get dirty," she says, explaining the delay, which she seems to have agreed to on our behalf.

"Well, if that happens, we will clean it. The important thing is to get them back in place so the house can start to warm up and dry out and we can move in."

I could tell Lucia was doubting our sanity. We were crazy to think we could move in before Christmas.

It's a month since we have finished sanding, undercoating and painting sixty window frames and three French doors. The Carpenter has done his part and now The Glass Man has them and has confirmed that the windows will be returned to their rightful positions 'soon'. The expensive tools the plumbers and electricians had left in the house overnight and over the weekends have not been touched, and neither have any of the dusty antiques we have held on to, so I decide it's safe for us to skip the iron bars on the windows.

26

OLIVE PRESSING PER 100 KG: €17

October is a busy month in Umbria. It's not only firewood collection time but also olive harvest season, and this year's crop is much better than the previous two years.

I have driven past Constable-style scenes of families sitting on the green nets under one of their trees eating their packed lunch having started at sunrise and still hours of work to go before they finish at sunset. I've seen a Nonna standing in the middle of a road holding up the side of a net as a matching Nonno precariously dangles off a wooden ladder reaching the sacred branches of their ancient grove's bordering trees, which must have been planted before the intrusive road existed.

The olives are picked and brought to one of the many olive pressing mills in the area on the day the crop is booked in. There is no time to waste and not an olive to be missed.

Giovanni has the 20 trees in the front garden stripped in one day. The next day, he arrives in a new white, shiny Lamborghini. I didn't realise olive oil was so profitable. I should point out it was a small Lamborghini tractor he was driving. Ronan asked how many miles on it.

"Three!" he responds, very happy with himself.

It had just arrived, and he had hitched his rusty trailer to it and driven directly to our house to take us up 'his mountain' on a firewood hunt as promised.

"I didn't know he owned 'a mountain' and I'm no expert on tractors but a Lamborghini anything would cost a lot," says Luca. "Do you make that much money from olive oil?"

"If his finances are as meticulously organised as his sheds and wood pile then that's how he can afford a mountain and a Lamborghini... or he inherited the mountain and Anto bought him the Lamborghini from all the money I've been paying him."

Being in debt to anyone makes me insomnia-level anxious. I don't like staying awake and I don't like being anxious, so I pay the lads promptly for their work. We have a system where Anto and Danny Boy create their invoices for the works done, we meet with Tomo and go through them in detail and then agree on the next set of work to be completed and the price.

Tomo magically turns up for these meetings and just stares blankly if anyone mentions him not answering or returning calls. The day after the meetings I go to the bank and make the payments using the special forms to claim back the renovation bonus.

Danny Boy is definitely not used to getting paid promptly. He keeps telling us how wonderful we are and says he'll put double the amount of electric sockets in the hallway where I want to put the Christmas tree. He thought I was joking and, like the others, he asked "which year?" I didn't laugh. Each time I see him I give him the countdown in weeks, days and minutes to when the tree will be going up on the 22nd of December.

The tree has now turned into a threat.

We follow Giovanni's rattly trailer pulled by his shiny tractor up the mountain and park outside a section of fenced and gated woodland. Walking behind him through the woodland, he points out neatly stacked piles of wood. We're not sure why we are being given a tour of the different deposits of felled wood, but the walk is enjoyable. Watching Giovanni getting very excited about a bunch of mushrooms, which he promptly fills his cap with, is even more enjoyable.

He goes into a long explanation of why he is so excited about these particular mushrooms and tells us not to tell anyone. No fear in that, as none of us understood what he said. He points to the smaller ones he'll come back for tomorrow when they will be much bigger. Maybe it's not just the olive oil that allows him to afford a new Lamborghini and a mountain. Maybe it's all the money he also saves by foraging for food.

We follow him back up to where the tractor is and load the large pile of seasoned logs, already piled near the gate, into the trailer. Giovanni definitely has OCD and I know he will have a particular way to stack them and sure enough, he does. Long pieces are propped up around the edges to form a fence as the fatter logs are loaded. We are quite proud of our stacking effort until we drive back down Giovanni's mountain and get stuck behind two tractors at different points with skyscraper-loads of perfectly stacked wood. One trailer has custom made metal holders for the supporting 'fence' sticks. I have firewood stacking jealousy for the first time.

We stop off at the Workhouse on the way back. One of the selling points of The Workhouse was that the plaster was sound in most of the rooms, so they would just need a lick of paint and there was no need for expensive re-plastering. It wouldn't take much to get it into move-in-able shape. Not anymore, unfortunately. Large slabs of ceiling plaster now lie shattered on the floor.

We also have a new variety of mould growing on some ceilings. This one is a nice orange tone to go with the autumn theme. Perhaps a rare edible fungi will now grow from the damp blackened walls which we can sell to Giovanni to fund all the re-plastering that will need to be done. One can only hope.

The builders seemed to have found a few more walls to pummel and drill, which I didn't think was possible. New mounds of precious walls are lying in rubble heaps.

"When will they stop destroying and start repairing?" I'm exasperated. Although Tomo has not been in touch, he has also not formally said he is no longer playing and we have no idea of the game plan anymore.

With eight weeks to go to Move-In Day, we need to know when the windows will be put back, so that I can tell the kitchen company the date they can install the units. We need to know when electricity will be switched on and if it will take as long as the water or the gas, which there is still no sign of happening. The evenings are getting shorter and we want to start painting the downstairs and tiling in the evenings after the work crew is finished.

"Can you please get back to me? I am really not happy about this," I text Tomo.

He doesn't respond. Two days later, Anto texts me and asked for a meeting. He suggests we meet at the farmhouse. I didn't know where he was talking about, so I suggested we meet at the Workhouse, only to find out later that the farmhouse is what they call the house we currently rent from his father.

He brought a friend to translate, a friendly girl from the village, and Giovanni. Which is weird as we just saw Giovanni up at our house and he didn't mention he was coming along. It's Sunday, so Giovanni is driving his good Sunday car, not his 40-year-old Fiat, and he is wearing a crisp white shirt.

"I heard you were disappointed with my work," Anto starts looking like he might start to cry at any moment.

"What? No! You have been the most helpful out of anyone."

Ronan and I are both shocked. This is the last thing we expected him to say.

"We know you have been delayed because of weather, but your guys are here every day working their hardest."

"But Tomo called me and said you had texted him and told him you were not happy. We know we will miss the deadline but we are doing our best after the weather," the girl translates minus Anto's hand gestures.

"No, no, it is not you, it is him. He does not return calls and has disappeared for weeks. That is what I am not happy about it. It has nothing to do with your work. We are more than happy with your guys."

Anto's feathers are smoothed. I still have no idea why he brought his father along. But then they express that they are worried about our optimism of moving in, in November.

"If it is an issue about money and not being able to pay the rent," says Giovanni, "then you don't have to pay for the final months."

"It's very generous of you, Giovanni. We are happy to move the move-in date to December, before Christmas. But I need the ground floor finished by then as I want to bring my mamma and papa to live in Italy as soon as possible."

As soon as the translator has repeated this in Italian, both Giovanni and Anto have their head in their hands, "Ohhh the Mamma e Papa!" They are both talking quickly to each other. Giovanni met my parents when they were over last year and treated them with the care and attention like he would his own. He brought my mum little gifts and always asks after them.

"Bring them to live in the other apartment beside you at the farmhouse, no additional rent," cries Giovanni.

"Again, that is very generous of you, but my mother can't walk stairs because of her back. There are no steps to the ground floor in this house, so it would be perfect for them. I need to get the ground floor finished. "

"If only we had known this, we could have waited to do the roof until next year."

I'm gutted.

"We could have waited to get the roof done?"

This was never put to us by Tomo as an option. The thoughts of not having that huge gulp of money taken from our restoration fund during a time when we don't know when work would start flowing again was a kick in the gut.

In hindsight, I am glad we did it when we did and didn't wait. The dirt and disruption after settling into the house would have been a nightmare.

"I will put an extra two men on the job to speed it up," announces Anto.

And that's exactly what he did. There are a gang of workers on site every weekday. All the scary stories I had previously heard about builders disappearing for weeks and work being delayed has been the complete opposite of what I have experienced so far – long may it last.

In the meantime, Ronan's chainsaw broke and we needed it for chopping up the firewood. He found a secondhand one for sale online through Marketplace in a town ten miles away. He began messaging the seller back and forth. It went on most of the day, using Google Translate makes each text take five times longer. Some of the messages he was getting back were translating as very formal and a bit weird. Eventually Ronan admitted to the seller "I'm Irish and can't speak Italian so I'm using Google Translate."

The response from the seller was; 'F**k no! I'm from Belfast, I can't speak Italian either and have been using Google Translate!"

A deal was soon struck. It needs to be sharpened or a new chain, but otherwise it seems like a good buy.

27

PELLET STOVE: €2400

Now that the house is semi watertight we focus on the next topic; heat. The radiators are being installed, but the gas connection, like the water, we have no control over. They will come when they feel like it. If you call them too much they will put you at the bottom of the list. That is what Tomo told me but perhaps he just wanted me off his back.

It probably isn't true. Anyway, the risk of us being put on the bottom of the list is very low as I would not have a clue what to say to them if I did call. I avoid telephone calls in Italian at all costs. To be honest, I don't know if the Italian number I got to open the bank account even works.

Tomo was most recently spotted at the olive mill, I'm guessing his phone was crushed under one of the stone mills as he still isn't answering it. I've resorted to asking everyone else on the crew about getting the gas connected and whenever I ask some progress is made.

A Rosie Life In Italy 2

For instance, I ask Danny Boy what we need to do to connect the gas and he tells me Anto needs to install a box in the garden at the front fence. I chase Anto and the box gets installed. A couple of weeks later I enquire about what to do about getting the gas installed, and Anto tells me the Danny Boy needs to install the pipes. So I chase Danny Boy and he installs the pipes.

A week later and I enquire again, with what I need to do to get the gas installed and Anto tells me the gas company needs to come and connect it. Okay, so it is in the gas company's interest to do that as they will have a new customer right? Wrong. The gas company will put the meter on to connect us to the public gas supply but then we need to contact the private gas companies to become a client and then when we decide who we will become a client of, then they will do the final thing, whatever that is, to get us gas.

So, one thing at a time. Anto has kindly given the public gas company a call on my behalf.

Someone told me they waited two years for their gas to be connected. "Get your plumbers to change the connection for gas cylinders and use it just for water heating."

A lovely woman who is following our progress on social media texts me; "Hello my dear, I hate to be a 'downer'. I waited two and a half years for the gas connection with the town gas pipe being right outside my door. Now I am not saying that this will happen to you... but the box and everything was there for a year before I actually got connected. BUT the good news is you can do practically everything with the bottles of gas. Your builder can connect them up so you can get hot water but don't use them for heating as they will be used up within a couple of hours. I used bottled gas for a year. I hope that your region is better than mine, but know there are alternatives that work."

I would be lost without expats on social media and my yoga group who have done all this before me. At least I now know that we need to be prepared to wait.

But then I get a text from Anto in Italian, which I am all thumbs trying to translate with my app; "the gas guys will be there between ten and 12.30 today, can you go to the house as they will need a signature?"

It is 9.45. I have not yet had my cornflakes, I'm still in my dressing gown and it takes me 15 minutes to get there.

I switch to high speed. Like the water connection guy, you don't want to miss the gas guy. They only appear every couple of months, apparently. This is amazing news, the gas connection is one of the major things that would get in our way of us moving in before Christmas, as we need it for the heating, hot water and to cook. Everything else is figure-outable.

I arrive and wait in the garden, watching the guys putting the last tiles on the roof. As usual, they have Moroccan trad music playing at high volume. The first time I heard it with my uncultured ear, I thought a few of the workers were having a huge argument on the roof. Meanwhile, the electrician has an Italian radio station blasting inside so he can hear it over his angle grinder. There's an unknown Italian song playing worthy of a Eurovision entry – loud, screechy and about unrequited love.

Today's Moroccan roof choice is much cooler than the one I heard before, it sounds like we are all being called to prayer.

A Rosie Life In Italy 2

I'm guessing the neighbours are praying that the roof will be finished soon so the daily international music festival at my house will stop.

It's three weeks past its finish date, but they did have the issue of having to build two new supporting walls inside the house and the combined two weeks of heavy rain days in September that also delayed progress.

I get a call from the gas guy. He's outside. I can't see a van. I go to the gate and a tall scrawny guy in his early 20s is standing holding a single piece of paper. He says something I don't understand, but I guess he wants to know where the gas connection is to go, so I lead him to the corner of the garden and show him where the pipe arrives from the road and where the pipe goes to the house.

I'm expecting a crew to follow him in. He stands away from me, obeying social distancing, and stares at the corner. "I see you have the tube-ees."

"Sí, I have the tube-ees. I need the box." I am tempted to say box-ees but resist.

He hesitates, I'm looking at him. He doesn't seem to know what to do, so we both stare at the tube-ees in the corner.

"I make a photo," he decides. "I make a photo outside too." And he goes back outside the gate, and then across the road taking photos. I feel I should be in them. He's on a roll, snapping away. The tube-ees are not that pretty.

He comes back. "I need your signature," he says, holding out the single piece of paper fluttering in the breeze.

"Ok. Do you have a pen?"

"No."

I'm glad he has come so well equipped for the only job he has to do.

I find a pen on the floor of my car and use the back of the car as a table. "When will the meter be installed?" I ask.

"I don't know."

"How long does it usually take? Days, weeks, months?"

"I don't know.... we send the documents to the gas company then they decide when to come."

"Oh, so you are not from the gas company?"

"No."

I am waiting for some sort of explanation of who he is but he gives me nothing.

"Good morning," he says, taking the A4 sheet from me and walking away rapidly in much shorter steps than his long legs would be capable of. I get back into the car and see him still walking at the same rapid pace towards the town holding the sheet of paper by its corner with his finger and thumb, at arm's length from his body like it's a dirty wet rag. I'm hoping that his distaste for the important piece of paper is from fear of COVID and not the fact that we haven't washed our car in about a year.

Who knows if we will have the gas turned on by Christmas? The guy at the gate definitely doesn't.

So, without a gas connection, we need a Plan B to have some warmth in the house for the winter. The next thing on our

A Rosie Life In Italy 2

shopping list is a pellet stove for the sitting room. Pellet stoves are covered by the 50/50 reimbursement scheme, while fittings such as the kitchen and bathroom furniture are not.

We go to the heating shop where Ronan is legend for going into it the first time and declared in Italian "I have a bomb" instead of "I need a bombola," which is a gas cylinder in Italian. It made people go quiet and they still laugh hysterically or probably nervously when he goes into the shop. I still think their hysteria is tainted with fear that he could actually be a terrorist. He is Irish after all.

The pellet stoves in Italy are weird. They tend to be tall, ornate objects coated in red, cream or green ceramic. The colours of the Italian flag. I have more of a simple taste. I just want a matte black square stove. They have one and of course it is twice the price of the more ornate ones, as the one I want is a German make, not Italian. Ronan tries to persuade me to go with one of the cheaper ornate ones, but even he, after looking at them for ten minutes in the shop, realises he'll hate it after an hour in our house.

We order our lovely stove. It will take 20 days to be delivered. I am starting to realise it takes delivery men 20 days to get to you no matter what you order in Italy.

'Prepare fireplace' is added to the list. It's one of those big old fireplaces, with a chain hanging down in the middle which has a big hook on the end to hang a cooking pot over the open fire. There are hooks on the sides up in the chimney where a griddle and triangular pot stand are still hanging.

We know we can cement the holes on the hearth to even it out for the stove, but we are at a loss on how to make the cracked and broken tar-covered rear wall of the fireplace look good. We start by scraping it. It makes little difference.

We plasterboard it with heat resistant plasterboard and tile it with brick tiles but then measure and realise the stove is so fat that it needs all the space, including the couple of inches the plaster board takes up. A precious hour of work is spent removing the work that already took half a day. Ronan sets about smoothing the ugly cracked and scarred back with cement and plaster with some success. I had it in my head that I wanted it all white as a background to our lovely stove, but then Luca walks in from going through one of Paolo's drawers. "Why not just paint it black?"

He has a point. I then get a brainwave to spray paint it black and it works. We have a very presentable fireplace ready to house our cosy stove when it arrives.

28

NEW TV: FREE

It's mid-November, usually a time that I start to feel Christmassy but instead we wake up to the announcement that Umbria will become an 'orange zone' from the next day for at least a month. This means that in 24 hours we will not be able to travel outside our area. Our plan was to check one thing off our long list every day to get us to the goal of moving in just before Christmas. Like an advent calendar countdown.

The house we are renting sits in Umbria, less than a mile from the Tuscan border. All the shops we need are in Tuscany. We've learned that it takes 20 days for things to be delivered after you order them in Italy. If we wait until the lockdown restrictions are lifted to shop for the things we need, the appliances and tiles won't be delivered until January because of the Christmas holidays in between. There is no solution other than a trolley dash for essentials to get the house fit to move in to.

It may have had a slow start, but this is now turning into an against-the-clock, high-speed renovation. It's like we have been told we need to eat all the cheap chocolate in the Advent calendar in one sitting. It makes my dream renovating a villa in Italy a lot more stressful than enjoyable. We still have not become like the couples you see on mortgage ads in matching overalls, laughing as they paint walls with artistically dabbed paint on their faces.

"We should split up," says Ronan looking determined over a quick breakfast.

"You might have a point. After 25 years maybe we could both do with a change."

"What? No. I mean about shopping. You go buy the tiles and paint, and I'll go buy the electrical appliances... what do you mean a change?" He slurped up the last of his porridge.

"I was only joking," I say gulping my tea. I was shocked at myself that for a fleeting moment, I had considered that swapping Ronan out for a handyman who could speak fluent Italian and English would be a good move for both of us for the next few weeks. Just until we got the house done. It would make life so much easier.

It was definitely more likely to happen than us splitting up to shop separately. The last time Ronan went out to get an electric appliance without me was 17 years ago. When he went out to buy a vacuum cleaner and came back with three live chickens.

I was pregnant with Luca at the time and at the nesting stage which involves non-stop cleaning.

A Rosie Life In Italy 2

"I need a bloody hoover that works," I said, struggling to vacuum up the drifts of dog hair that wafted off our previous dog.

Off Ronan went. An hour later, I heard the car turn into our driveway and I stood at the front door feeling very confused as to why Ronan was having a pillow fight with himself in the car.

He had seen a sign for chickens for sale on the way to the electric shop. We had said we would get chickens someday, which to me means probably never, but to Ronan it means as soon as possible.

So Ronan returned from his vacuum buying mission with bales of wire and three chickens and no vacuum cleaner. The chickens had escaped from their box, and were swooping around his head, possibly trying to gouge out his eyes as he drove.

"It will be great for Izzy to come out in the morning and collect eggs. I can't wait to see her face."

He spent the rest of the day building a high-tech chicken pen, burying the wire into the ground and attaching to what was our brand-new tool shed, now converted into a chicken coop.

I decided it was best we stick together this time to avoid any more Jack and the Beanstalk episodes.

We've been to this electric store many times in the last six months and have a good idea of the appliances we want, but no final decisions between brands. Ronan and Luca have been eyeing up a massive TV for months. They stand and stare at it whenever we are in the shop.

"Why would we need such a big TV?" I always ask.

"My sight is getting bad..." answers Ronan. But when that doesn't work he says, "Think of the children", as if they are both going die of hunger if they don't get the TV.

"We're not getting a new TV," I state as we walk into the electric shop for our trolley dash. I don't know why I bother saying it. I know we are going to walk out of there with a new TV, if our budget allows. The one we have seems fine to me, but to Ronan, watching a small TV is like asking him to stick pins in his eyes every night.

We're short of time and quickly discover that playing Top Trumps with the electric ratings is the best way to decide; Ronan stands at one side of the aisle at his fridge choice while I am on the other with mine.

"What's your freezer capacity?"

"240 litres"

"Mine's 210."

"Fridge Capacity?"

"300 litres."

"Mine's 330."

We're neck and neck. It's down to KW-per-year energy rating. I take a chance and chose Energy rating "A+".

"Ha, mine's A++, two out of three mine wins!" he shouts.

Using the Top Trump method, we have both the fridge and washing machine ordered within five minutes.

The strong football magnet in Ronan's head has dragged him over to the TV aisle to watch a match while I go to pay.

"There's a special offer at the moment, three for two," says the guy at the cash desk who speaks English. "If you buy a third item you get the cheapest one free, so is there something else you need?".

I had already glanced at the price of the lusted-after TV walking in, and I already know it is cheaper than the washing machine by €20 so it will be 'free'.

"Perhaps a TV," I say to the sales guy. He walks with me over to the TV section. Ronan is glued to the game.

The football match is playing on all the display TVs, except on the TV I know that Ronan and Luca really want which has mouthwatering drone scenes of a beach and a yacht.

"We'll take that one," I say to the guy. "The one with the yacht and the beach. I don't really like football."

He's not sure what to say to me. Ronan overhears me, "What? We're getting the TV?"

"Happy Christmas, love." I say, knowing that he can't understand the ads about '3 for 2' over the intercom. He's elated but then instantly looks worried. I know he's thinking about how he's going to have to come up with an equally good present for me. I point at the TV to give him a hint. Crystal water lagoon... yacht holiday? But no, he hasn't taken the hint, he's too excited about the TV. I'll probably get a vacuum cleaner... or chickens.

It's weird trying to renovate a house during lockdown, as we have to buy a lot of stuff online. I feel like I am living in a cave with a severe shopping addiction as I try to order Christmas presents for all the family I won't get to visit pre-Christmas. Part of my perfect Christmas vision is a pile of thoughtful, perfectly wrapped presents piled under the tree. Perhaps some I have made myself throughout the year. But that won't be happening this year, the presents I am ordering are a bit random, along with the house stuff, there is a very mixed jumble of things being ordered. Amazon's 'Customer's Also Bought' algorithm is having a meltdown and doesn't know what to offer me.

In the last month alone, I have bought ceiling lights for the hall, varnish for the front door, a picnic basket, a roll of tropical wallpaper with parrots on it, knickers, socks, a board game, one stuffed rabbit, black bathroom taps and an old broken sewing machine. The only urgent thing that is left on my list to get is a shower tray.

You'd think finding a shower tray in a shop in Italy would be easy, but it's not. With the range of shops in our catchment area limited, I can't find what I am looking for and every time I step into our half-bath dribble shower, I am reminded that time is ticking and I need to find a shower tray.

I start searching online for a suitable shower tray, but I get distracted and I end up buying a book and two nighties for my mother, woodworm treatment and wallpaper paste. Only later I realise I didn't check which address each individual order was going to; my home address in Ireland or my home address in Italy? Order dispatch notices are merrily popping up on my screen at a rate that I can't figure out which order it is and which address they are going to. There is a decent chance my mother is going to get a bag of wallpaper paste

A Rosie Life In Italy 2

and a dose of woodworm treatment for Christmas, while I will have some very nice flannel nighties to wear while chopping wood with our new chainsaw.

However, within a week, the nighties arrive with the woodworm liquid to us in Italy. And our first water bill. I've never had to pay a utility bill in Italy before. We just give all bill payments to Giovanni. As I have to pay it in the post office, I decide I will be super organised and post Christmas cards this year. I have years of well-intended written cards stacked in the Christmas decorations box – I never made it to a post office in Ireland to buy stamps in time to send them. Instead, I usually ended up taking a photo of the well-intended card and emailed it to friends and family. This year I will surprise them. I will not only send them Christmas cards, but parcels as well.

I wrap my Mam's Christmas parcel in a reused delivery bag, lots of tape and a shabby homemade label. The parcel looks worthy of a rubbish dump rather than under a tree. Of course, I don't intend to send it like this, I am going to buy a large jiffy bag or nice box at the post office and re-parcel it there. This one is just going to be a liner, as I haven't seen any postal packaging for sale anywhere.

So off I go on my bill-paying postal adventure. There is a queue with everyone spaced out a meter apart.

The opening hours of the post office are 9.45 to 12.35 on Mondays and Wednesday and some other set of obscure hours on other days. I think they do it to confuse people so fewer people will turn up on the right day at the right time. The queue moves slowly for the first hour, but as it approaches 12.15, they start to fly through people. It is eventually my turn. I say in my best Italian I need to pay this bill, and I would like to send a parcel.

The payment slip is cut from the bill with scissors. Her face tells me she has been sucking lemons for breakfast. She runs it through a machine and, several ink stamps and staples later, our first utility bill for The Workhouse is paid.

"And I would like to send this."

I have to go up to the door at the far end of the room and put the parcel in. It is left in an airlock room before being removed on the other side by someone else.

"You want to send this? Are you sure?" She is looking at the parcel in dismay.

"Do you have boxes or bags?" I can't think of the word for envelope. And I definitely don't know the word for padded envelops.

"No!" she looks at me shocked as if to say why on earth do you think we would sell packaging for things to post?

She weighs my shabby parcel, prints out a heap of franked stamps, and sticks them on the front. Now I am the one looking in dismay at the Christmas parcel my mother is going to receive. Perhaps she will be so overcome with surprise at me actually sending her something that she will overlook the state of it. I have to fill out a docket about what is enclosed and my sender address. She reads it out of nosiness and is visibly disappointed that I have written it in English, which she can't understand.

"Also, I would like to buy some stamps. Ten for Ireland and three for the US."

"I can't sell you stamps. We don't sell stamps." She looks at me twice as perplexed as when I asked her for packaging.

I am beginning to wonder if I have walked into the right place. Glancing around, yes, there are posters featuring happy people and Poste Italia written on them. I am not in a butcher shop; I am in the right place, although I can't see happy people like the ones in the posters. All three counter staff have the same expression as Mrs Citrus on the other side of the counter.

"You don't sell stamps?"

"NO. You need to bring what you want to post here and then we decide if we can send it for you."

I am sure she means we can then decide how much is needed to send it for you. Although judging by my experience so far she probably has the power to decide she can't send a card if she doesn't approve of the colour of the envelope.

"They are just Christmas cards. Standard weight."

She now thinks I am clearly just wasting her time and it's five minutes to her three-hour lunch break. "No madam. Stamps in the tobacco shop if you want them. Or bring the items here."

I leave proud that I sent my first package and paid my first bill but somewhat disillusioned that I could not buy stamps.

So I drop into the corner shop to see if I can get stamps. Corner shops in Italy don't sell chocolate, candy, crisps, cans of sugary drinks like they do in Ireland or the UK. Actually, sugar loaded stuff for kids is not as freely available here, I've only seen them for sale in small sections of the supermarkets.

It might explain why I haven't seen overweight kids in Italy. Maybe there are obese kids in the cities, but I can't recall seeing any. Kids here are out on their bikes, eating home-made meals and slurping gelato for their sugar fix.

Corner shops here are tobacco shops that sell cigarettes, an array of scratch lottery cards and kids' toys for some reason. They often have a couple of gambling machines in the back too. I think the logic of selling kids' toys is that they are probably licenced to sell 'games' and that's how they get away with having the slot machines.

"I want to buy stamps to send Christmas cards," I say to the guy who looks like he just played the part of 'tough prisoner 1' in a movie.

"Sí! How many do you want?"

"Ten for Ireland and three for the USA."

He has a book of stamps out that all look the same. "Oh, we only sell stamps for Italy."

"So how can I send cards to other parts of the world?"

"You go to the post office..." He sees me deflate.

"Or you can just put four of these stamps on each. It should be enough."

I go with the 'chance my arm' four stamp option, rather than the bitter lemon option. Just as I am leaving it strikes me I haven't seen a post box.

"A silly question. Where is a postbox around here?"

"There is a yellow one outside here, but don't use that. They never collect from it. There is a red post box in town outside that estate agents, use that. They often collect the mail from it."

This whole palaver makes me realise why greeting cards are not a big thing in Italy. Birthday cards are very limited in choice and, again, difficult to find. Greeting cards are something I'd normally go to a newsagent for in Ireland. Hallmark has not got its grips on Italy yet.

I go home and stick the stamps on the envelopes. And realise the woman in the post office was probably right to insist that I go into her. She must have known my type and saw me coming. She knew these cards would be lost at the end of a house move box and never see the inside of a postbox without her assistance.

29

CHAINSAW SHARPENING €3

Ronan found a local guy who sharpens chainsaws. He was sitting outside after his lunch.

"I will have it done in three days. It cost €3."

His wife comes out screaming at him to get off his lazy ass. He reluctantly leaves his sun chair and has it done in 15 minutes.

In every house we have owned, I have tiled kitchens and bathrooms, floors and walls. I am not an expert, but once it's straightforward and I get my centre point, level line and tile spacers, I find it fairly easy. The blue hexagonal tiles with the geometric pattern are beautiful and, depending which way you lay them, you can form different patterns.

In the online magazine picture, they are on the floor and continue up the end wall and on to the ceiling of the shower area. The room is only 8' x 4'. The end wall has a tall window set back in the thick stone wall with an alcove underneath it. The wall on either side of the window inset, is only a hand-width wide running from floor to ceiling.

The shower will be at the end of the room in front of the window. I explained to Joseph this is where the shower will be and I intend to put a shelf in the alcove. He translates to Omaroberto, who asks questions which Joseph translates into, "You like tiles in the shower?"

"You will have water here?" He's asking these confidently with hand expressions pointing at the floor and ceiling. I nod, realising Joseph's command of English is worse than my Italian. He's winging it. I also realise in that moment that Omaroberto is actually the senior foreman and not Joseph, as we originally thought. He's winging it to impress his boss. Omaroberto is waiting for my answer to his important question, which I am sure was not about if I liked tiles in the shower or if I will have water in the shower. But I like Joseph, so I play along and nod with a serious "si, si."

Joseph is delighted. His success has put him in a particularly chatty mood.

"When is the tile man coming?"

"There is no tile man. I am tiling it."

He looks confused. "You are bringing the tile man?"

"No, I am doing the tiling."

"Ah, your husband is tile man?"

"No, I am doing the tiling."

He continues to look confused.

"What job do you do?"

"I plan weddings."

"Oh, you play weddings!"

I give up.

I switch the subject and tell him I am looking for a particular type of shower tray that is very thin as I want it more like a wet room, so it will be easy access for my elderly parents in the future.

"Ah yes, I sit here for your Mamma and papa when they shower." He crouches into a seated position.

It takes me a little while to figure out that he doesn't intend to sit there and watch my mother or father shower, but he is indicating that he understood I wanted to leave room for an aide seat for them in the future.

Two days later, I come in to discover Roberto has built a shelf into the alcove made from wood and plasterboard. It's not what I wanted him to do at all and it's completely impractical and just more corners and messy pieces of tile to cut.

But instead of ruining Joseph's reputation as the English expert on the building team, I decide to pretend I'm just being a fussy woman who has changed her mind and ask them to remove the shelf that I am sure took Omaroberto ages to build.

The lads have also built a plasterboard wall on one side, as it has been too pummeled by unnecessary plumbing channels to plaster over directly. It is this wall that will house the slim, mysterious cistern with the ball cock that will never stick.

The online photo I have saved to my mood board has plain white tiles on the other two facing walls, and that is what I am going to do. With the plumbing and plastering completed, I spend a few hours finding the starting point for my wall tiles and the level for the first row. I wait until the lads have gone home and then mix the first batch of tile cement and start on the wall. The white tiles go up relatively easily and the hand tile cutter I bought snaps the half tiles I need perfectly in two with a little applied strength.

I leave the second wall, ready for tiling the following day. At this rate, I will have the bathroom finished in a week.

Luca is nearly finished sorting through Paolo's drawers. He brings down what looks like a silver coin. It has Garibaldi on the front and a lion on the back with writing, saying something about a centenary. Luca is on the case researching; "It's a commemorative medallion marking the 100th anniversary of Garibaldi's birth, I think, possibly Argentinian. There's one just like it but in better condition for €45 on eBay. Should we sell it?"

Although €45 would cover the cost of a wash-hand basin, I'm thinking it would be a shame to let the house's treasure leave its four walls. Or what is left of the four walls.

"Let's keep it for now. We're not that desperate yet. If things get bad, we can start selling stuff off, but don't worry, I don't think we'll get to that stage."

I arrive the following day just as the lads are going for lunch. They have built a small, makeshift barbecue in the garden and it seems Joseph, with his insulated picnic bag, brings the homemade dishes every day for them to dine on. They sit at one of the tables and chairs they have brought out from the house for their alfresco dining experience underneath the apple tree.

When I arrive, they are just downing tools and Joseph says, "Ah, I see the work of your husband. It is very good."

"Thank you. I did it though."

He nods, still convinced he's misinterpreting something.

I mix the cement. Five tiles into it, with my back to the door, I hear footsteps pause at the open door and then speed up to outside. Another five tiles later and all the lads are walking casually past the door and looking in as they pass. Joseph pipes up, "You do it? You do tiling in Ireland?"

"Only in my own houses."

"Many women do this in Ireland?"

It's not a question I know how to answer. I mean I don't know the percentage of Irish women who have tiled a wall but I know there are plenty who have risen to the challenge or would give it a go, so I just decide to throw a spanner into his concept of what a woman should do and say, "Yes, lots."

The three of them are standing at the door watching me work. One is eating a sandwich. I feel like a zoo animal.

Three hours later and I am nearly finished with the second wall. Ronan has cut two small sections out for the shower pipes on one tile I have marked up and I've slotted it in and continue up the wall. The lads are getting changed, packing up their picnic basket and tidying their tools away, ready to go home for the evening. They all pop by to say goodnight, but linger to come in and inspect my work. They are looking at each tile as if it's an exhibit in an art gallery.

Omaroberto comes in and looks at the tile we've cut to go around the shower fitting. He shakes his head and talks to me in Italian, making hand gestures about the tool I need to make round holes.

I shake my head to explain I don't have such a tool. Translation master Joesph is now in the room and saying, "Holes should be round."

"Yes, I know, but I don't have a tile drill bit that size."

Omaroberto is banging his chest like Tarzan.

I just nod and smile and wish they would get out of my bathroom and stop judging my work. My wish comes true. Joseph returns later and brings me in a cup of tea before he leaves.

I tile for another two hours and then finish up for the evening. I have had to find a technique of rolling sideways on my bum and straightening my legs slowly as my numb knees feel like they are going to crack. I don't remember this happening the last time I tiled a floor, but that was twenty years ago. Jeepers, I am getting old.

At home, I soak my hands in warm water. Tile cement makes your hands raw and nails brittle. It also embeds deeply in around your nail beds, so if a brittle nail breaks at least the impossible-to-remove cement keeps it in place.

The following day I come back to get started. There is a tile with two perfectly round holes cut out hooked on the protruding shower pipes.

The blue tiles are not so easy. I should rephrase that. The blue tiles are an absolute pain in the ass. They are thicker, so much more resistant to being cut by the tile slicer. Also, seven varieties of shapes have to be cut due to the alcove wall and ins and outs of the floor. I leave those to do last. It takes me a whole morning to find the perfect starting point which involves bits of string, chisels and hammers acting as weights, levels, chalk and finding bits of wooden slats with straight edges. I get the first half of the floor done on the third day and the second half on the fourth.

"You don't stop for lunch?" The Italians and Moroccans are horrified at my non-stop work ethic. Joseph brings me in a cup of tea in what is now my own tea-stained, grubby builder's mug. He has gone to the bother of bringing milk with him just for my tea. By now I'm considered one of the team and they seemed to have forgotten I am the owner who wants to move in to the house in a matter of weeks. That is why I don't stop for lunch.

Omaroberto plays traditional Moroccan music all the time when he is working. I think it motivates him to work faster. I know I've found myself tiling faster as the tempo of the music coming in through the window from the roof speeds up. He's a dedicated Muslim and tunes into what seems to be a call to prayer channel from time to time, today was one of those days. He had arrived early and had the second replacement wall half built and his prayer channel belting out just as Ronan arrived.

"Jaysus, the neighbours are going to think we're building a mosque," he says, looking up at the foot-thick, solid wall Omaroberto is building.

Several times I have walked out to the garden to find Omaroberto on his makeshift prayer mat made from a slab of insulation foam board, doing his daily homage at the east side of the house. I've also walked into the garden several times and had to divert my line of vision away from one of them peeing at side of the shed. I definitely won't be paying that €1000 for the non-existent Portaloo.

30

TRAIN FINE: €66

"They can't stop Christmas, can they?" Luca asks during our daily check of COVID updates.

The number of COVID-19 cases is rising again in our region and I'm getting worried about rumours of a lockdown for Christmas.

"No one can stop Christmas. The only thing that would stop Christmas for us is if Izzy couldn't make it home. But that's not going to happen." I am saying this with determination but also apprehension, as it is mid-November, and I have heard of a possible new mutation in the UK. My instinct is to tell Izzy to come home sooner, but she has friends near her for the first time in months and they have created their own bubble and new ways of socialising with 'Come Dine with Me', style dinner nights and game nights. It's such a relief to see her happy again with a sense of hope.

Izzy's work contract has just ended and the lease on her flat ends next week on the 26th of November. I wanted her to fly out the day after, but she wants to spend her birthday with her friends. She has flights booked back to us for the 9th of December with an open-ended ticket for a couple of months. I'm trying to not let myself get excited, with lockdowns things can change at the drop of a hat, however we have everything covered so the excitement of us all being together again for an extended period of Christmas movies and hot chocolate curled up on the sofa is making me work faster on the house.

"Mam, now don't be alarmed when I say this but.." Izzy says on a call while packing up her apartment. "... I can't find my passport."

Days of searching and a whole series of stressful calls to the Irish Embassy and a closed passport office in Ireland ensue. The passport office will reopen in Dublin on the 2nd of December. Because of COVID, only emergencies are being dealt with. A young female with an expired lease on her flat and nowhere to go during a pandemic is not an emergency, apparently. Eventually, a Maggie in the passport office gets back to Izzy and tells her to order a new one. Which she does.

The following day, Izzy calls. "You are not going to believe this, but I found my passport. It was tucked into the back corner of my wardrobe shelf under my suitcase."

I am sticking my fingernails into the palms of my hands, resisting the urge to say something cutting as that would have been the first place I would have looked had I been there.

"That's great, so you can come home on that and cancel the new one."

"No, unfortunately, the new one cancels out the old one. Maggie at the passport office told me yesterday, I am not to try to use it as it is now cancelled. But she also said that my new passport is on its way. It will reach me just in time for my flight home to you, so don't worry."

It's a relief to hear this. The same day, Italy announces a new rule, instructing that we need to stay in our commune from the 22nd of December to the 7th of January. We not only need Izzy back by then but we NEED to be in the house by the 22nd, otherwise we won't be able to get to it until January. This is not an option for me. By January, I need to have my work desk set up in a warm room ready for bombardment, as January is the busiest admin month of the year for a wedding planner. All the excited, newly engaged at Christmas couples jump into the challenge of planning their big day.

Not only that, but with the rise in cases around the world, some couples are already hinting at possibly moving their wedding date again to the following year. I have persuaded them to wait until the New Year before making a decision, so I am going to have a lot of anxious clients wanting me to predict the future of the pandemic come January. I can't handle the thought of what will happen if we have another year like this one. It's too much to think about. Financially it would be disastrous for us, it just can't happen.

I know for sure I am not going to have time to do anything else as I usually spend 12 hours a day answering emails throughout January and I want to spend any spare moments with Izzy and us as a family, not moving and renovating. We decide that, as soon as the windows are in, we will start moving our stuff up to the house.

A couple of days later and we are reluctantly leaving the warm rental to go down to the new house while the wind is howling outside and shaking the trees of all their remaining leaves. We are exhausted from our rigorous Workhouse schedule, my legs are like lead and if they could talk, they would be screaming at me not to go. As would my shoulders. Actually, every part of me is reluctant to go, but in my mind's eye, there is a Christmas card image of how things will be if we keep pushing on, so my limbs drag themselves on. I wrap up warm, gather my tools and open the front door of Giovanni's, only to be greeted by a complete mess.

The wind was so strong that it blew over a tin of black gloss on the terrace. I'd been so careful not to get any on the terrace tiles when doing up the shutters and lamps, and now the formerly full tin of paint is creating a mini replica horror version of Lake Trasimeno on the terrace. I don't have time or the heart to clean it up. We need to be at the Workhouse as I have had a string of early morning text questions from Super Mario. I throw a cleaning rag on top of the paint and hope I will be in better form later to clean it up.

"Oh crap, I seem to have forgotten my phone. I was sure I had it with me." I search around the floor of the car just as we pull into the driveway of the Workhouse. I can't find it but I have no time to go back home to get it. Everyone seems to have questions and issues about something that needs an answer before they can continue what they are working on. Joseph, Mick Kelly, Danny Boy and all the Marios.

I feel stupid and helpless all day because, without my phone, I can't translate what I need to say. Without my phone, my tongue has been cut out. I was feeling exhausted before we even got to the house and by the time it's dark my head is pounding and I feel like my body is made of fine bone china, teetering on the side of a very high ledge.

By the time we get home, the winds that have been howling for the last 24 hours have decided to go for gold and up their game to storm level. I search the house for my phone and then search the car again, but more thoroughly this time in case it fell out when I got in that morning. I definitely had it leaving the house as I had read the slew of texts from the workers in the Workhouse. Ronan calls my number and I can't hear it. I have the hearing of a bat, so if it was in the house I would hear it. Even if the ringer was switched off, I would hear the vibration. It's nowhere. I'm too tired. I'll find it in the morning.

Luca started college a few weeks ago. The second day of going on the train into Florence he comes in the door with the words, "Did you know you have to carry ID with you in Italy all the time? I got an on-the-spot fine on the train for not having ID."

"How much?"

"Sixty-six euro."

He's laughing about it, I'm so angry I could burst. That's at least four tins of paint.

Because of COVID, all his classes are online so no more chances of fines. One of his lecturers has given them a list of recommended movies to watch. It includes 'Chainsaw Massacre'. I know he is in third level and not in kindergarten, but it still seems an odd choice of recommendation. I think they are following how special effects have developed. It has never been a movie on my 'must watch' list, I have to admit, and after a long frustrating day working on the house, I lug myself off to bed and leave the lads to watch the movie.

Just as I am going to bed, I remember the tin of black gloss paint blown over on the terrace, but the storm is really starting to kick off and I am too tired to deal with it in the dark. I'll do it tomorrow.

I take Ronan's phone into bed to call Izzy. Asha, as usual, plods in to the bedroom with me. She's limping a little.

"You're getting too old to be running up and down the fence with Nancy," I say, petting her floppy ear gives both of us comfort. She is the perfect height to pet beside my bed, where she sleeps every night.

"Now don't be annoyed," Izzy starts with. That's never a good start to a phone conversation. "My new passport arrived in England... but they didn't deliver it. They said the address was incomplete. I've been following the tracking all week and yesterday it was in the local post office and today I noticed it was back in a sorting office at Heathrow."

As Izzy was out of her own place now, she had given her friend's address where she was staying until she got a flight to Italy. "The Royal Mail decided the address was 'incomplete' because I didn't have the number of the flat on it. They put it for automatic return to sender without even trying to deliver it. There are only six flats in the house. The post is left in the porch for all of them, it could have still been delivered. I thought they would call or something... They have sent it back to Passport office in Dublin."

"Oh Izzy, how could you be so careless? Of course they didn't deliver it, you didn't have a complete address on it!" I'm screeching down the phone, "You are in London, not the friendly backend of nowhere in Ireland or Italy where the postman knows everyone. I took Omega-3 oils when I was pregnant. You have a high IQ. How could you be so stupid with something so important as this?"

"I told you not to be annoyed at me!" She's upset and getting all my angst build-up of the day.

"Bloody hell," I say exasperated. I really don't want to be annoyed at her because of what tomorrow will be, so I try to backtrack.

"It's an easy mistake. Look, there is nothing we can do about it tonight. Call the passport office again in the morning and see what they say." I'm trying to calculate in my head if she'd still make the flight in four days' time if the passport arrived back in Ireland in the next couple of days and then gets sent back to her again–but my head is wrecked. I can't think anymore. I need to lie down and rest. I'll think about it tomorrow.

I am awoken from a deep sleep by a huge, prolonged boom. The house is trembling, the windows vibrating. Then, there is a woman screaming hysterically. In my confused state, I jump out of bed and run out to the front door to see what is happening. It's a classic Italian storm; buckets of rain, booming thunder, fork lightening worthy of any horror movie along with accompanied hysterical screaming. Well, the screaming is not usual.

The lads are chuckling at how bad the movie is. This is where the source of the continuous hysterical screaming. I'm still standing at the open door and one cat runs in soaking wet. I look down to see if the other cat is around and there it is; my phone, in a puddle beside the spilled lake of paint. The paint-soaked rag has blown off and stuck itself on the terrace wall, decorating more of the tiles in black gloss.

I hesitate to pick up my phone, because I don't want to find out it is not working. Without it, I am mute. A perfect crap ending to a crap day.

I bring in the dead phone and stick it in a box of rice as I have a vague recollection that's what you do to dry them out. I'll look at it tomorrow, I say to myself, and go back to bed. My positivity battery is running on low. It needs to be recharged more than the phone.

I fall asleep to the woman screaming continuously. I wonder how much they paid the writer of the script who just must have written pages and pages of "AAAAAAHHHHH."

"At least I am not being chased by a maniac with a chainsaw," I mumble to Asha, strangely comforting myself at the thought. However, at this stage I feel if I don't go to sleep soon and get this day over with, that could still happen.

31

ACID (5 LITRES): €22.64

Ronan must have discovered my phone in the rice before he went to bed and, I am guessing by the hairdryer out on the table, that he had taken the time to demolish my phone, dry it out and put it back together again. It's now slowly charging, the screen looks faint, but it seems to be working, which is a relief as I need to distract myself today.

It's lashing rain, so I'm not dealing with the spilled paint yet. I'm hoping the rain will wash it away or at least keep it soft until I have the heart to deal with it. I'm dreading going up to the house to see how our alfresco non-windows have coped with the storm.

Tomo was spotted on the roof of the supermarket recently by Lucia. He was wearing a tool belt, so we presume he was working and not jumping. Both Lucia and Mick Kelly feel responsible for his lack of work as they recommended him, so they are helping out with issues that Google Translate can't handle. I need to get things back on track, so I start the day with determination and text Mick Kelly; "We need windows before the kitchen arrives. Please, can you get on to the carpenter and ask him to bring back at least the ground-floor windows this week?"

"Okay, I will have an argument with the carpenter."

"I think you mean discussion?"

Maybe he did mean argument at this point, as both Lucia and Mick Kelly have been trying to get The Carpenter to set a date, to which his answer is always "don't worry it will be done." No one seems to respond to this with "Yes, but when?"

I'm still annoyed at Izzy for being careless with an address for something so important. But I'm more annoyed at not being able to be annoyed at her as it's her birthday today. It's a significant one as it's the first one we've been apart and she's 24 which is the age I was when I had her. And I remember thinking I'd be 48 when she is 24 and wondered what we would be doing then.

I imagined we would be together having a big party with lots of friends and family around, presents galore and Christmas decorations festooning staircases, hallways, and a cosy fireplace. I never thought I would be biting my nails in Italy over a missing passport while trying to get her back to us during a worldwide pandemic.

However, I have enough distractions to keep me occupied; the plumbers, who were working on getting the waste pipes connected to the sewerage system, are surprisingly, not on-site today and neither are the electricians, so we can start working on other rooms without feeling like we are in their way. This week we aim to finish prepping the walls of the room for the kitchen and we need to start on the sitting room and hallway and get the windows in. I'll come back to the never-ending bathroom tiling in a couple of days. I can't face it, I need a break from tiling. My positivity battery is charging slowly but not fast enough to face tiling.

I make the kitchen red brick wall my project for the week. It needs all the loose mortar removed, acid scrubbed onto each brick and scraped off, new mortar applied to the gaps and then the whole thing sealed against dust and for easy cleaning.

There is still no word on the passport. The tracking is still showing it in Heathrow. The angst and stress we are all feeling isn't helping. Izzy eventually gets to speak to someone in the passport office. It's the Maggie woman again and she says Izzy has to wait until the new one is returned to the passport office. This means she won't be flying on Wednesday.

There is an extra growing challenge –Italy is currently seeing the highest number of COVID-19 deaths since the end of March and the Prime Minister has told Italians to expect a "more sober Christmas, without Christmas Eve gatherings, hugs and kisses."

Many Italian regions are under partial lockdown and the beloved Italian Christmas markets have already been banned.

In the short term, this means we can't leave our region to go to the big DIY stores to figure out what 'sealant' is here or find a nylon cleaning head for the drill, which would make the job ten times faster. For the next couple of days, I keep myself and the red brick wall amused with a scrubbing brush and five litres of acid.

The extent of the Christmas travel ban is being increased. People will not only have to stay in their regions over Christmas, but they will not be allowed to leave their homes on Christmas Day, Boxing Day or New Year's Day. No travel will be possible outside your home, never mind regions from the 21st, so Izzy has to get here by then.

Izzy, Ronan and I pull together a new plan. When the passport arrives back at the passport office in Ireland, we will ask them to send it by courier back to London. Izzy books a new flight for the 15th and we just hope that the flight doesn't get cancelled. She reschedules the mandatory pre-travel COVID-19 test and researches what the new rules are for travellers to Italy after the 10th, that's if she gets her passport and gets the flight.

Who knows if Izzy will get her passport in time for her flight. The Maggie in the passport office is definitely not the one who can tell us, why would she know? And no, Maggie says, it is not possible for anyone to collect the passport on Izzy's behalf from the passport office. She would need to collect it herself.

"But I'm stuck in London without a passport."

"Well, that doesn't matter anyways, as you can't collect passports at the moment due to Covid," explains Maggie.

"Okay, so we will order a courier to collect it when it arrives back?"

"No, it is not possible to have a courier collect it. You can only collect it in person."

"But I'm stuck in London without a passport."

And so the conversation goes round in circles. Maggie has noticed its Izzy's birthday and wishes her a happy birthday. Izzy bursts into tears. The passport tracking is still showing Heathrow.

"Forget your passport for the rest of the day. There's nothing more you can do today. Get ready, go out and enjoy yourself," I say, consoling the baby I held in my arms for the first time this day 24 years ago. Her boyfriend has booked a table at her favourite Italian restaurant in London, so at least she will have a flavour of Italy on her birthday.

The faith of our Christmas spirit now lies in the hands of some unknown higher powers in Italy and a Maggie and a few others in Irish Government offices.

I might join the lads on the roof for a prayer session later to see if that will help.

32

ELECTRIC BILL 2 MONTHS: €145 (524 KWH)

There are no electricians or plumbers to be seen for the second day in a row. We arrive at the house after being at the bank where I have paid our first electric bill and transferred a chunk of money to the plumbing and electric company. Ronan is looking concerned. I can see his mood plummeting to that depth of thought neither of us wants to go to that involves the words 'there's no way we are going to be in here by Christmas'. I've heard of tradesmen disappearing for months after being paid, and for us, every hour is crucial in the next four weeks.

The roof lads are milling along, they are lifting the tiles on to the roof. They have finished building the two new retaining walls that were wafer thin and have the stonework done on the side of the house that had previously looked pretty ugly. I had considered whitewashing it and doing a Banksy style mural on it, but I suppose stonework might be more acceptable to the facing neighbours.

"Where are the plumbers and electricians, Danny Boy's crew?" I ask Joseph, who is in the garden heating up some water on their campfire.

"I don't know," he says, bewildered.

"They will never finish this in time for Christmas." He did it. Ronan verbalised the unspeakable.

"Why you want to move in so immediately?" Joseph addresses this to Ronan and is also verbalising the unspeakable. He has become comfortable enough with us to have friendly chats rather than owner and worker discussions, and has said what a lot of the workers have muttered to each other. Even with my weak command of Italian, I picked out enough words and shoulder shrugs to figure out they think we are missing a few marbles.

He asked Ronan something similar the week before and the week before that. The last time he stated matter-of-factly, "But it will just be you moving in, not your wife. It is too dirty for your wife." I don't think he was worried about my extensive wardrobe of work clothes getting ruined by the dirt. I think he was more concerned that I would have a nervous breakdown in my wifely duty trying to clean it. Either way, he was finding it difficult to comprehend that Ronan would allow me to move in to such a dive.

"Do you want to answer this time?" Ronan is smirking.

I shrug. I don't know how to say or how to admit that we will be out of money as soon as the roof, windows, and plumbing are done. We can't afford not to move in and there is a certain type of anxiety that sets into your brain when you commit to move from one place to another. You could be very happy in the place, overlooking the faults and making the most of where you are in that moment and then as soon as you are moving to somewhere better, you can't help but focus on all the bad things in your current situation.

That was us for two years in Giovanni's rental. We didn't really notice it was a house of hallways for the first year. Five hallways, in fact. Three bedrooms, a kitchen and a bathroom. That house got us to Italy, and we were grateful for it.

To us, it was so much better than the place we had left behind in Ireland. Even though the place we had left in Ireland had much better central heating, an electric shower, it had a modern kitchen, although small, two bathrooms and more rooms. But our rental in Italy was so much better because it allowed us to get to where we all wanted to be; Italy.

We were happy. We saw all the pros and how lucky we were and overlooked the faults. Then we found The Sighing House and now it was getting closer to the reality of moving in. We were getting impatient with the small kitchen, five cold hallways and dribble shower of our rental.

The next day, we drive by again. The roof lads have their Moroccan music belting out, as they are now more than halfway through the tiling. Again, there are no plumbing or electrician vans to be seen.

"Bastards have taken our money and ran," says Ronan, who always thinks the worst. He gets a sniffle, and he thinks he's going to die of pneumonia. A pandemic has not been a pleasant addition to his fatalist mentality.

"Maybe he pulled them off-site until we paid the last invoice?"

I am the optimist in our relationship, so I text Danny Boy: "I made the payment yesterday morning. None of your guys have been here for the last few days. Is there a problem? We are anxious to move in the next four weeks."

He responds nearly immediately.

"Thank you for the payment. True, there have been no guys at the house for the last few days. One worker was not feeling well and we have to wait for his tampon to come back."

The fact that they call COVID tests tampons here is still weird to me.

"We will be back on Monday if all is well."

We go back to Giovanni's and try to distract ourselves for the weekend. On Sunday the worst news text arrives; "Two workers have tested positive for Covid."

"Which guys are they?" I am holding my breath, thinking of how we have been working in close contact with the workers. We have tried to stay aware, but sometimes we have let our guard down. Ronan, being diabetic and over 60, is not a suitable candidate for COVID.

"Well, here's the thing... you were in contact with them."

I try not to panic. But I'm finding it hard to text with my trembling fingers and tightening chest. Project managing texting in a language you can't speak is not straightforward. I need to write it in English in Google Translate then reverse translate it to ensure that by putting an 'o' or 'a' in the wrong place, I haven't mentioned a vagina or penis instead of drainpipe or nail.

"Which guys are they?" I am not only worried for us, but worried that it might be Mario One or Mario Two, both of whom are overweight and older.

"The two young apprentices, they are okay, they are just showing mild symptoms," is his answer. That is a relief. We had passed them in hallways, but that was over ten days ago and we were not in the same room as them for more than a minute.

He texts again, "I cannot let the crew work for ten days. I do not know what we can do yet, I will let you know on Monday."

This is not good news. I haven't thought about creating a Plan B if we couldn't be in the house by Christmas. I just wasn't allowing myself to go there, but I have to face the fact that we need to figure one out. The only option we would have is to take a temporary apartment in Lucia's Agriturismo.

One apartment would not be big enough for four adults, so we'd have to divide ourselves in two. That would mean no turkey, as the holiday apartments don't have an oven, and the Wi-Fi wouldn't be strong enough to get our TV working. While I am resigning to the fact Christmas in the house may not happen, I am thinking Christmas in any form we know might not happen either.

The roof guys are a separate crew so they can continue working. A gale force wind wakes us on the Monday morning following Danny Boy's COVID bombshell. I get up late and reluctantly; I want to just go back to sleep and wake up when this is all over. There is no way the roof guys will work today and no workmen on-site when we are on countdown would just be too depressing.

"Come on, let's go up to the house and at least try to finish the bathroom tiling. I'll work on finishing the kitchen room prep." Ronan is always better and more positive after eating lunch while I just want to nap, but I reluctantly pull on my tile-cement-encrusted jumper and follow him to the car.

But as we round the corner to the gate, our driveway is far from empty. Not only Joseph's car is there, but a van from Danny Boy's company.

Banging is so loud we can hear it before we enter the hallway. Two electricians we haven't seen before are feeding cable through the black plastic arteries imbedded into the walls under the stairs where I imagined the Christmas tree. I text Danny Boy. "Your guys are here?"

"They are a different crew who have not been working with the young guys. If we have to work day and night, you will have your Christmas tree lights!"

While I have been texting, Ronan has gone upstairs to see what is happening. "They couldn't work outside today, but they have nearly all the interior scaffolding down!" he exclaims excitedly, bouncing back down the stairs.

A new energy floods through my veins.

I push on with tiling the bathroom. It is still taking forever. Lucia calls in with a flask of water so that we can make tea and coffee. She's looking at my tiles, I can see she's not impressed. I'm covered in tile cement.

"In your defence, those tiles did look really good on your mood board," she says munching on a biscuit.

"They'll look better when grouted. ... I'm so slow at tiling! I've another three days' work to do on this bathroom. And I can't find my fishy drain covers."

Ronan is passing by, he has been staying away from the bathroom as he knows I like to work solo on a project at my own pace, but he must have heard from my voice that I was losing the will to live.

"Come on, let's get the bloody bathroom finished. I'll help."

Ronan cuts the difficult shaped tiles for the bathroom floor corners, a job I've been putting off, but now with Ronan's help, I feel we can tackle the awkward bathroom and get it finished before the week is over. It's not long before it's too dark to do any more and Joseph and the crew give us a cheery goodbye after nodding their approval at our tile cutting.

As soon as the lads are out the gate, I'm up the stairs. I walk around in the darkness with my torch. The house may have no windows, but, with the interior scaffolding gone from the rooms, it feels cosy. It feels like a home.

Being an emotional, hormonal, midlife-crisis woman, my face creases up and hot stingy tears burst through. Ronan has followed me up.

"Are you crying?"

"The scaffolding is gone!" I blubber.

Now that the rooms are empty, I can walk out onto the first-floor balcony again. The trees are stripped of their summer greenery and I can see the silver face of the lake, its ripples winking at me. We have a long way to go, but there's a glimmer of hope again that we will cook the turkey and watch Christmas movies in the house. With that thought, I take a deep breath and sob even more.

Ronan puts his arm around me and says softly, "I didn't realise you liked scaffolding so much, I'll buy you some for Christmas."

33

BOTTLE OF BEER: 80 CENT

It's three days before the kitchen is due to arrive and the builders have put in the new lintels to stop the two floors above collapsing on our heads. The new lintels take an extra two inches' of space from the door height. With the help of his ever-growing legs, Luca's head of curly hair now grazes the underside of each doorway on the ground floor.

"Now that the lintels are in," says Ronan, "we can start playing that game we've been waiting to do – Which of the missing doors fits the hole." We soon realise this game is not fun, and I am regretting not making the previous owners get the nine doors they stole the weekend after we put down the deposit for the house, rehung.

The doors are Madonna doors. The door frame attaches to the outside of the doorway like a picture frame, and the door slots on to the receiving hinges, like a cap over a finger of metal. The doors are all different sizes. After a few false starts, we develop a technique.

We number all the doors with their corresponding frames and then unhook the frames which we run around the house with trying to find the corresponding hole. Ronan, with his "It will do" attitude, tries to convince me that some smaller frames fit perfectly in spaces that are just that bit too big for them.

After several "No it won't bloody do" arguments and having a last frame on the second floor that completely doesn't fit the space left, we have to start again. Eventually, with all doors sort of fitting, pure exhaustion has me agreeing with Ronan's "It will do" argument. We also realise that the frames, when originally put in place, were attached to wet cement.

The door thief was not gentle, so large chunks of the cement and plaster came off with the frames when he was prying them off. Secretly, I note to myself that we will probably buy new doors next year after we get the walls re-plastered. But for now, they'll keep the growing winter winds somewhat at bay, so they will do.

Having the place sealed up also means we can start painting the kitchen and clearing the floor space for the kitchen to be installed.

We are working on the sitting room and kitchen until the light fades, which is earlier each evening. However, eleven days to move-in and there is a game changer.

"Now you can have your Christmas tree!" exclaims Danny Boy as he flicks a switch and lights on the ground floor come on for the first time. I let out that weird screech of delight again that hasn't been around for a while.

A Rosie Life In Italy 2

"This means we can work late into the night after the builders have gone home." Ronan is trying to sound excited by this, but I know he is secretly as pissed-off as me that we can no longer use the excuse "It's getting too dark" to go home earlier when our bones and every muscle begin to ache.

"Tell you what," he continues, "once the stove arrives, why don't we move our mattress here and stay here after dinner a few nights so that we can get an early start as well?"

"Great idea." I am sure he can see by my furrowed eyebrows that I think this is a terrible idea. My sciatica has kicked in big time and I can't stand up straight, leaning lopsided and bent forward. I am focused on getting home and scrubbing the tile cement off my raw hands before falling into bed.

"I was going to suggest that I'd start to stay up here anyway because the appliances are being delivered soon. We can then move our computers in and get them set up... We need to get new locks on the doors."

We still don't have a working shower or kitchen, but coming back to stay over makes sense after we eat and shower at the rental. We can't move the cats in until the constant flow of workmen tramping through the house with their muddy boots stops. We'll need to keep them in for a few weeks to get them to feel at home. The cats, not the workmen.

The first night we have lights, we work late to finish the kitchen ceiling and get the three walls painted and the red brick wall stripped of all the cement lumps with acid and an electric wire brush.

Since the COVID scare, we try to wait and arrive after the builders have left. By the end of the week we are exhausted both mentally and physically, but we have a meeting with Mick Kelly after lunch, so we make our way to the house a little earlier than our recent usual. We arrive to see beer bottles lying in the garden beside deck chairs.

"Oh no, are there field drinkers in Italy? Is someone using our place to have night parties?"

"Ah, this is a good sign," chuckles Mick Kelly. "It means they are finished the roof, they had a topping off ceremony. Usually it is when the last beam is put in place, but I think because they were under such pressure to get this roof finished for you, they have waited until the last tile was put in place."

"Look," says Ronan, staring at the house. I was so distracted by the beer bottles I didn't notice. "We have windows!"

All our painted windows with double glazing are in place. It is as if some magic being has come and waved a magic wand. My mood has suddenly escalated above anything that I have felt in the last couple of weeks.

With ten days before move-in, the house is weatherproof.

But my mood starts to plummet again as I jog from room to room, opening and closing windows gently, only to discover it's not possible with some of them. Ten of the refurbished windows won't close, not even close to closing. I mean, resisting to close even close enough to latch them closed. I might be the one having an argument with The Carpenter this time.

"I'll fix them," says Ronan.

A Rosie Life In Italy 2

"No, you won't! We have paid him good money to refurbish these windows, you are not doing his work for him."

"Oh, bloody hell, he'll probably not be able to come out again for weeks and that will mean we can't secure the house enough to start leaving stuff here. It's a pain in the ass hauling the tools back and forth every day. We're constantly leaving things behind. I'll do them."

"Before you start demolishing the windows could you message Lucia and ask her to tell The Carpenter's daughter that he needs to come back and fix the windows so they close, and let's see what he says?"

The Carpenter arrives within two hours and says something about coming back with his son to fix them all. He says his usual line "Don't worry, they will be done," but, as usual, doesn't indicate when.

I'm feeling frustrated and pretty low about the windows being so ass-ways, but consoled by the roof being finished.

There is still our wheelbarrow on a pulley on the scaffolding outside the second floor, dangling above the front door. It looks like we are intending to fill it with hot olive oil to pour on intruders. Our new shiny copper gutters are all in place. Ronan has a walk around the scaffolding.

"This is one gorgeous roof. Maybe we should build a staircase so we can just come and admire it now and then, it cost us enough."

We scrub the floor tiles in the kitchen with acid. They are coloured cement, hexagonal tiles from the 1920s. They are flawed but I like them. Ronan is not so fond of them but agrees that if it saves us a couple of grand not to replace them, then they are nice.

The kitchen room with windows is looking great. I text the kitchen guys and say the room is ready when they are.

But there is little time to stop and admire our work. Ronan immediately starts working on getting the sitting room into a finished state, while I continue working on the bathroom tiles. I just have to grout them now. That shouldn't be too problematic, right?

34

BABY JESUS: €6.99

"When can you come?"

"We are here."

"Where?"

"At your house, we are nearly finished."

"Oh my God Ronan, the kitchen guys are at the house, let's go."

It was only 11am–and our beautiful kitchen cabinets were all in place, along with a corner hood and corner stove beside the red brick wall. The matte black sink was set into the black marble countertop. They were finishing the island when there was a knock on the window and a van reversing into the drive.

"Delivery of a fridge and washing machine."

I'm looking blank, as he says it in Italian and it takes me a few moments to translate it without using my app.

"Ah yes, sì, sì, perfect timing!"

They manoeuvre the fridge into place and leave the washing machine in the sitting room until the electrics are finished in the pantry room. Just as they are leaving, The Carpenter arrives with a guy to fix the windows. He explains via my app and Joseph that he would need to file the windows to make them close.

"Okay then do it."

"He doesn't want to do it as they will shrink in the summer and there will be gaps."

"But they won't close? It's getting bloody cold."

"I know but he does not want you to have gaps."

"I would prefer to have gaps in the summer than having the windows swinging open in the winter."

He files the minimum amount off, forces the windows tightly shut and tells me in Italian with hand gestures not to open the windows. He didn't tell this to Joseph. Within an hour of The Carpenter leaving, Joseph and the crew have opened most of the windows.

The kitchen is being fitted. We have our appliances and there is a digger in the garden, clearing the rubble. The Moroccan guys who built our roof and have worked so hard to make this place our home are clearing all the rubbish from the garden. There is hope again. But there is still one thing missing: Izzy.

"Has your daughter got her passport yet?" Joseph asks when he finds me mixing a batch of tile cement to get the bathroom finished. Omaroberto comes in. Shaking his head, he leaves the room. I thought it was because he is so appalled by my technique, but he returns with his professional cement tile spreading tool from the back of his van and gives me a demo of how to do it. He asks Joseph in Italian about the passport and Joseph answers with a sadder tone than I could have done.

"I will pray to Allah for help," he smiles as he hands me the spreader.

The electrician is wiring upstairs, someone is using a Kango hammer somewhere for something. I have no idea why at this stage.

Mario, one of the plumbers, asks about the passport. I give him an update. He'll pray to Saint Anthony.

The house is buzzing, there is music everywhere, everyone seems happy, the sun is shining and I get a gush of love. They are helping us build a beautiful place and the house is starting to wake from her surgery.

A quick visit to the DIY shop is extended as I browse the rows of shelves dedicated to the Nativity. Growing up in Ireland, the Christmas crib stood on the hall table – a cave scene made from a black plastic bag over a biscuit tin usually. Our family had the same set of crib characters since my mam and dad got married. In the 50 years since, the sheep had lost all their legs, one of the wise men had been beheaded, and baby Jesus had both his outstretched arms amputated.

In Italy, nativity crib building is a big tradition. A nativity scene can take up most of a room, illustrating the happenings of an entire village at the time of the birth of Christ. The DIY shops have rows of shelves with characters and craft stuff to help bring an extraordinary scene to life. Next year, I'm going to build one in our hallway. This year I'm just focusing on having a semi-finished hallway.

Building the Christmas crib was always my job when the decorations came down from the attic each year. I swaddled baby Jesus in toilet roll to hide his stumps and decorated the garbage bag cave with fresh ivy from the garden. It was naturally my job, as I was going to be a saint. My Catholic upbringing had me convinced that being a saint was my fate, and I studied, as much as an eight-year-old could, the requirements to achieve the role.

My favourite movie was 'The Children of Fatima' and, while others had posters of pop bands on their wall, I had prayer cards, novenas and a hologram picture of the Virgin Mary whose eyes followed you when you walked by.

During my 'studies' of saint lives, I learned I was probably going to die young, see visions, and I would end up wearing barbed wire in my underwear for God's approval. The pay off? I would have statues made of me and a Saint Rosie Day.

I spent quite a lot of time figuring out what I would be the saint of. Naturally, I wanted to be the saint of animals and I had a secret jealousy of Saint Francis, as he already had that gig. But then I decided I could be the female version, and he was put back up in my favourites. I thought animals would start talking to me when I became enlightened. This was the other bonus of being a saint.

A Rosie Life In Italy 2

I thought I had it good in Ireland with all the saintly Catholic stuff available to me; we had the moving crib, Saint Valentine's Heart in my granny's favourite church in Dublin and Oliver Plunkett's head in a church in Drogheda. But travelling around Italy has made me realise how much weird stuff there is about saints that eight-year-old me missed out on. I'd have been in my element growing up here.

For instance, during a work trip to Puglia, I was walking down a little street and passed by a church dedicated to Saint Lucia. There was a painting of her above the door holding a silver tray with a goblet on it and two... I couldn't figure it out and I said to the guide, "ha ha they look like eyeballs."

"They are eyeballs. She was pledged to be married and her suitor admired her eyes, so she gouged out her eyes and offered them to him on a platter as she wanted nothing to become between her and her devotion to the religion."

"But in the painting she still has eyes?"

"Yes, I suppose it would not look so nice if she has plucked out eyes."

In all the paintings and depictions of St Lucia she looks pretty and sanctimonious with eyes on a platter and eyes in her head. A miracle indeed.

Dante, the father of the Italian language, is said to have prayed to her to save his sight, and when she did, he included her as a character in his great literary work 'The Divine Comedy'. Amongst other groups, she is also the patron saint of electricians and glaziers. I will be probably praying to her a lot. Lucia means light and, as the bearer of light in the darkness of winter, her feast day is 13th of December. I find this out on the day they turned our electricity on, which happens on the 13th of December.

Another saint who is celebrated in December, who lived around the same time as unlucky double-eyed Lucia, was Saint Nicholas. Probably the most famous saint in the world. Like Lucia, he is also celebrated big time in Puglia but not just in December, his big day in the city of Bari is on the 9th of May.

I was in Bari during early May one year when they were preparing for his festival. Huge structures were going up that would light up the whole of the outside of the cathedral. But that was not what I found amazing. Inside the cathedral, a full orchestra was rehearsing for the two-hour mass that takes place on his feast day. I stood in awe as the acoustics whisked my emotions in every direction. If I could hear this regularly, it would make me want to become Catholic again.

"So why do they celebrate him in May? Is it his birthday?"

"No, it is the day San Nicolas' bones arrived here from Turkey," explained my Italian friend who worked as a tourist guide in the area. "Many thousands of people come to Bari for the two days of celebration. A gigantic statue of San Nicolas is brought from the basilica in a boat and embarks on a day-long sea voyage with a flotilla of dozens of boats. In the evening, the harbour is lined with thousands of people waiting to greet the statue's return. The statue is then carried on the shoulders of costumed men with flower poles and torches.

"At the end of the mass in the basilica, the choir chants and a priest crawls into the crypt of San Nicolas' tomb and brings out the manna."

"What the hell is the manna?"

"It is a liquid that always accumulates around the relics, the bones of San Nicolas, and while the choir climaxes, the vessel containing the manna is lifted for all to see. Then the faithful queue to be anointed with the manna."

I was curious, to know how they 'retrieved' the manna. Did they have to climb down steps or a ladder to get into the crypt? Did they come out muddy? So I Googled it and found a YouTube video of the event. Without being disrespectful, I always look at these things from the point of view of someone who knows nothing about the Catholic religion and walked in from the street.

So in the video, there is a group of priests standing around an altar. One of them ducks under the floor-length tablecloth of the altar they are all standing around. He roots around for a while, like he dropped his wallet during dinner after too much wine and he's looking for all the coins that fell out and rolled under the table. He comes out holding a small glass vase with about half a glass of clear water in it. The guy with the purple hat – the bishop – on the other side of the table looks very happy that his friend has found his wallet and holds the glass vase above his head and everyone looks very pleased with themselves.

I fell down the Google rabbit hole and started reading about how the bones ended up in Italy when he was laid to rest in

Myra. In turns out his tomb was a popular place of pilgrimage in Myra. Because of the many wars and attacks in the region, some Christians were concerned that access to the tomb might become difficult. For both the religious and commercial advantages of a major pilgrimage site, the Italian cities of Venice and Bari vied to 'get' the relics of Saint Nicolas.

In the spring of 1087, sailors from Bari conned the monks of Myra to show them where the remains were and succeeded in 'spiriting' away the bones, bringing them to Puglia. The shrine became one of medieval Europe's great pilgrimage centres.

So, basically, the sailors conned the monks into showing them where the bones that attracted all these pilgrims to the area of Myra were, stole the bones and brought them to Puglia to create a popular pilgrim site to attract visitors... like a medieval Disneyland?

I do like the stories around Saint Nicholas. The basilica in Bari has a special wedding donation box. The collection from the box is annually given to one couple each year who can't afford their wedding. This comes from the story of a poor man with three daughters. He had no dowries for the girls, which meant instead of getting themselves a good husband, they would be sold into slavery and prostitution.

Mysteriously, on three different occasions when each of the daughters was going to have to leave the following day, a bag of gold appeared in their home – providing the needed dowries. The father waited up the last night and saw it was good old Saint Nick. His parents died during an epidemic when he was young, leaving him a lot of wealth. He believed in giving to the poor and in need.

The bags of gold he tossed through an open window, are said to have landed in stockings or shoes left before the fire to dry. This led to the custom of children hanging stockings or putting out shoes to get gifts from Saint Nicholas.

There is another story of him reaching out of the sky and grabbing a stolen boy by the hair and bringing him back to his mother. The old masterpiece paintings depicting it are quite hilarious, but not such popular Christmas card material as Christmas stockings. Although I think I will use it next Christmas when I have more preparation time and if I can figure out how to send cards without having to visit the woman who sucks lemons in the post office.

We have done all we can do regarding Izzy's passport. I buy a baby Jesus in the DIY shop to start my Nativity collection and I've added prayers to Saint Nick and Saint Lucia to my daily to-do list alongside grouting. We have God under different names being asked to help and numerous saints on the case so all angles are covered.

If Izzy can't get back before Christmas, there will be some reason we don't know of at this moment, and at a later point in our lives we will realise why it was best. But it is all looking good again at the moment.

Now that they have fitted the kitchen and we have water, electricity, windows and a roof, the time has come to start to move stuff in. We elect a room to sleep in. I won't call it a bedroom... more of a space... a space decorated with mould. Van-load after van-load, we bring boxes, bags, suitcases up to the house and, to the dismay and amusement of the builders, we fill the big rooms upstairs.

Thankfully, my childhood urge to achieve sainthood was replaced with a longing to be a writer. But that is an impractical career choice, isn't it? Best to do something else. Maybe sainthood would be easier.

35

BAG OF STOVE PELLETS: €5.99

On the 10th day of Christmas my builder gave to me, an unwrapped house!

We arrived up at the house in the afternoon and nearly all the scaffolding was down. It was such a surprise. I really wasn't expecting Anto to actually have it done before Christmas, but he did.

The stove guys call. They will arrive with the stove later in the day.

Ronan is working on the sitting room's scalloped ceiling. It's the sixth coat and the fifth brand of crap paint he has tried and it's still peeling off in chunks to reveal the previous flesh-coloured paint. By the time it's dark, he has adopted the method of using the wet paint to keep the painted chunks and flakes on the ceiling to give a general impression of whiteness.

It's after 8pm. We are bloody cold and tired of waiting for the stove. We're just about to go home when a truck pulls in and, with a special hydraulic trolley, our 150kg stove arrives. It turns out the guys are just paid to deliver it, not install it. With several aching muscles, Ronan and I embark on getting the stove unwrapped and into place using bricks as mini scaffolding and stepping it up into the raised hearth of our big old fireplace. I have left the hook and chain to the side where pots were once hung to cook food over the open fire. I've also left the wire that runs under the mantle that was used to dry clothes from.

There's a manual the size of the bible.

"Right, we'll bring that home to study tonight and then give the stove a go tomorrow."

I go back to finish cleaning up the tiling before calling it a day, and within ten minutes, Ronan is calling me with glee. "It's great look."

He had lit the bloody stove for the first time without reading the instructions. He's like a kid with a new toy when it comes to things like this, whereas I'm an instruction book fanatic.

The following day is Friday, and after the workers are gone, we bring in the mattress.

The house is no longer topless. It has the most secure and most insulated roof on planet earth, but it needs a good session of heat to dry the walls out fully and help them recover from all the rain when the walls of the top two floors and a lot of the antique furniture got saturated.

A lot of the rooms in the house have now got what the Italians call 'humidity'. To me that sounds kind of tropical but it is the same as what we call in Ireland 'bloody damp', and it's

A Rosie Life In Italy 2

going to take more than a coat of paint to get them back in shape. Italian houses don't have wall vents, instead you keep air circulated by the woman of the house opening the windows for an hour in the morning while tidying and airing the beds.

That's obviously not going to happen in our house. But even without me developing Italian nonna housework skills, the walls have already started to dry out, which results in a growing variety of moulds on the wall.

So far, I've counted four: The 'common black spot', which is a permanent inhabitant and will only be moved if you take away the plaster. There is the 'black splodge'. This can easily be wiped away but smears and leaves the effect of a dirty protest by someone being held against their will in the room. Then there is the 'rusty brown'. This variety likes to make more delicate patterns which give birth to the 'fluffy white stuff'. The 'fluffy white stuff' grows in any unreachable spot and falls like snow when you do swipe at it with a long-handled brush, for example.

By the end of the weekend, we had slept in four rooms. This was not out of excitement or curiosity, it was to escape the humidity, i.e. damp. We slept in the sitting room the first night as we were too tired to assemble the bed. The pellet stove was flaming with the lorry load of pellets Ronan had bought to get us through the winter but seemed determined to use up in one night – it was cosy going to bed. The room seemed to go into shock from experiencing heat in ten years and with just a mattress on the floor, the intense stuffiness made it difficult to get off to sleep. Also thrown into the mix were the two dogs. We brought them down to enjoy their first night and see if they liked it. Of course, they loved it. The mattress on the floor was for all four of us to sleep on, surely? So with a giant German shepherd whose old bones were glad of the bed as much as ours and our bouncy Looney along with stuffiness, we got limited, broken sleep.

The second day we cleared out all the old furniture and books that were being stored in the room we wanted to be ours, even though it was one of the worst affected by the damp.

The more we cleared, the harder I found it to breathe. We thought with some electric fan heaters the room would warm up and be ok. But halfway through the second night, neither of us could stand the damp smell anymore, so we moved across the hall to a box room.

Moving room was not a simple task. It involved clearing the room of remaining rubble, getting knotted in drapes of dirty cobwebs so thick you could use them like rope, scraping cement and plaster off the floor, then sweeping and mopping it at least three times just to get to the point of being able to make out the pattern of the floor tiles.

Then we drag the mattress in and the bed base across and try to make it look like somewhere we could sleep. The box room is easier to heat with the electric heater, but there is nowhere for clothes or our stuff.

Early on the Monday I suggest we move into the other big room, which we've used as a storeroom for big furniture and all the stuff we moved from the first room. It has a built-in wardrobe and fewer ecosystems on its walls and ceilings than in the other rooms. We're not sure why we didn't consider this room first.

So we haul all the stored dusty stuff from this room back into the initial room we moved it from three days previously. We bucket the rubble, scrub the floor, sweep the walls of traversing cobwebs and wipe the years of dust and unidentified dead insects and mini skeletons from the inside of the warped-doored wardrobe. It's dark brown veneer and as ugly as hell, but the storage space is great and with a bit of a makeover, I'll make it work.

I add it to my ever-growing list of to-dos for the summer, when we will be out of our current survival mode.

It's only when we are finished setting up the room and plonk down on the bed that we realise we can see our breath, it's bloody freezing.

36

INTERNET PER MONTH: €35

"We need to fill in your holes."

"Nooo, you are not to go near my holes," I shout back. It's not the first time I have had one of these weird conversations with Mick Kelly. Today we are having a review of progress and what we need to get done for the house to get a certificate of habitability or something like that. I think he has said at some point we need it to move in to the house but I'm not going to ask him to elaborate on it.

"I like my holes. They've been there forever. Why do you feel the need to fill them now?" We are talking about the alcoves in the three rooms that were once kitchens in the apartments which will now become bedrooms. I have visions of making them into nice inset shelving units for books and candles or a wardrobe space.

"Rosie, it is better for the seismic level of the house. If it was straight bricks, it would be okay, but the walls are stone, so they are irregular and with movement, holes are dangerous.

A solid wall is safer than a wall with a hole. Holes in the wall make the structure weak and you have a lot of holes already for windows, doors and fireplaces. We need to fill in the unnecessary holes for safety."

What he is saying is that, in the event of an earthquake, the house is less likely to crumble on top of us if we have more walls and fewer alcoves.

"But we live here beside the lake where there are no earthquakes," I grumble.

"Yes, the lake does protect us from earthquakes, but there is still potential of movement."

I still find it a little magical that the lake somehow absorbs movement and protects us from earthquakes in such a seismic-prone country.

"When the lake dries up and drops below a certain water level, the surrounding land moves a little and can affect the structure of the house," he explains patiently.

"I don't think there's any fear of that. Have you seen the front garden? It looks like we've moved to Venice."

The watery theme around the house has been caused by the unusually heavy rainfall and exaggerated by the fact that the roofers and plumbers were not watching what each other were doing, so the roofers put one drainpipe on the far corner of the house and the plumbers put the ground drain inlet hole in the near corner of the house. The realisation that never-the-two-shall-meet only came about when the scaffolding came down.

This is noted in Mick Kelly's notes. Mick Kelly speaks some English, but Anto speaks none. He just goes by my facial expressions and hand gestures and understands perfectly. I'm rolling my eyes behind Mick Kelly's back and Anto is laughing.

We walk into the room where we had put our mattress earlier that morning.

"You are going to sleep here?" asks Mick Kelly.

"Yes."

"But it is dangerous," he says, pointing to the plaster that has been chipped away to put in the new wiring for the light. "It needs to be filled, otherwise pieces could fall, and it is heavy."

I find enough Italian to say, "It is okay, it is over Ronan's side of the bed."

Anto is laughing again but Mick Kelly isn't having any of it, "I am serious, it is dangerous!"

"Okay, okay." I roll my eyes again. Anto agrees to get Omaroberto out to finish filling the ceilings asap.

Ronan has found time to move his desk and computer into the second floor back room with the balcony. The black fungus is so bad in there that it looks like the inside of a cave. But he doesn't care about that, he is excited because today the internet guy is coming. Finding someone who can install fast internet has preoccupied Ronan's every waking hour for the last two weeks.

Carlos, the internet guy Ronan found somewhere, is delighted to speak English. He is taking giant steps around the house and having a great laugh with Ronan about something. Looking out the window I see Ronan holding the ladder as Carlos and one of the electricians climb into the neighbours' garden. The neighbour, who has only introduced herself by reporting us to the police for not cutting the grass before we had even bought the house, is not in.

"Shhh," says Carlos seeing me at the window. "We need to steal access to the phone line from their box."

"Is this something illegal?"

"No, it is just more fun if we pretend it is."

Fifteen minutes later he has the electrician drilling through our foot-deep wall with the Kango hammer to feed the phone line through. Carlos' booming laughter can be heard over the noise of it in intervals.

Within an hour he is finished with the installation.

"We have 100 megabytes." Ronan is practically wetting himself with excitement, but this means nothing to me until I open my laptop and everything pops up without any delay. "We only have 5 megabytes at Giovanni's, this is great, when we watch a film the words will be in sync with their lips now."

This will be a novelty. We haven't seen a movie with matching lips and words in ages. It will also be great when work starts again in January, all I need now is a home office... but that won't be happening for a while.

Later that evening, when everyone has gone home, me and Ronan are laughing about how safety conscious Mick Kelly is about the plaster falling off the ceiling. "As if that would happen?"

As if on cue we hear a crash upstairs. It takes us a while to find where the noise came from and then we walk into the room Ronan has set up as his office. A large piece of plaster has fallen from the ceiling and smashed all over the computer and printer.

"Maybe Micko has a point." Ronan's relieved his computer is still working but we are not too sure if the printer will ever be the same again.

"Well, at least it saves us knocking off the old plaster."

We quietly cross the hall and move our bed to the box room. Sleeping around has a very different meaning to us.

I text Mick Kelly to say they can fill my holes. I'll buy a bookcase.

37

FLIGHT FROM LONDON TO ITALY: €33

There is no sign of the passport arriving. The tracking shows it is still in Heathrow's notorious black hole sorting office. We ring everyone we know who might know someone that can help, but it's down to the passport office.

The Maggie at the passport office tells Izzy to order another new passport, as the first one is now deemed as lost in the post. Izzy will now miss her second flight. As it's getting closer to Christmas, flights are getting expensive and more difficult to find. Lots have been cancelled because of COVID restrictions, so she books another flight for a week later. I feel the timescale is too tight. As the passport office won't send the new passport by courier, it would take a miracle for a new passport to be issued and to her by regular post on time to get a flight on the 19th of December.

We get a local politician involved back in Ireland. They help us get authorisation to have my niece pick the passport up on Izzy's behalf. Her cousin can then send it by courier from Dublin so it doesn't get stuck in Christmas post. Solution found. We just need the Passport office to notify Izzy when the passport is ready for collection. This way she will make the flight.

In the meantime, the friend she is staying with is leaving London to be with their family for Christmas. Luckily they are kind enough to let Izzy stay in their apartment until her flight.

She has nothing else to do other than try to get through to the Passport Office every day to see if it is ready for collection. Each time she is told by auto message that the waiting time is 45 minutes and when she does get through after each 45 minute wait, the person either hangs up or there is an auto message to say the lines are too busy and cuts her off.

She emails. On Tuesday, they email her back. They have dispatched her passport... by post... to my parent's house in Ireland. We feel like screaming as every minute counts. Why didn't they let us know so it could be picked up?

I'm fighting back tears all day while whacking the last of the tiles onto the wall. Every last bit of hope is draining from my body about my girl getting home this week.

It's not just because of Christmas I want her home with us. There are so many more elements. Her accommodation situation is in limbo and the pandemic in all its glory restricts everything she can do socially so she is very isolated. Brexit is happening on the 31st of December and could host a whole range of problems for people trying to fly out of the country.

I've only seen her once this year, when normally it is every second month at least – I desperately want the two weeks of Christmas time when we forget about work, forget about the

A Rosie Life In Italy 2

last nine months of loneliness and sadness. I just want that warm, cosy Christmas feeling with twinkling lights, making nice food and watching stupid movies in our new old house. I want us all to feel 'home' here.

Four days until move-in and the radiators are being installed and a hot water boiler arrives for the Star Trek operations room. But the boiler has a broken bit, so it is being sent back and Danny Boy assures me a new one will arrive in three days. That is cutting it bloody fine.

The piles of rubble are starting to be removed from all the rooms in the house by Omaroberto and Joseph, and the hall is starting to be cleared of their equipment and tools.

Thinking about the passport all the time, I realise I tile faster when stressed and have the tiling finished by the end of the day. Two Christmas cards arrived from home; one from my parents and one from my brother Jim's family.

Christmas cards have never meant this much to me but looking at the word 'love' in the familiar beautiful cursive handwriting of my mother – the same handwriting that wrote sick notes and excuses to get me off PE class, signed test scores, report cards, birthday cards for the last 47 birthdays, told news from home during my travels, helped me write my first book ideas down when I was ten in front of the fire on a spare school notebook – the words 'love Mam' in her handwriting fill my heart more now than any other time.

My chest and throat are rigid with the amount of emotion they are holding back. Izzy will probably miss the flight as there was very little chance that her passport will arrive by post overnight to my parent's home in Ireland, I miss my daughter and I miss my Mam.

The following day I start grouting. Joseph is first in to inspect or admire what I am doing. I am using icing bags to squeeze the grout into the gaps between the tiles, a technique I saw on Youtube. At first he laughs and then he sees how effective it is.

"But it is slow."

I am happy with slow and neat. As lunchtime approaches, Omaroberto walks past and gingerly places his professional grouting paddle inside the door and nods a smile. He gives a quick demonstration that makes it look easy, and it would be a lot quicker.

As with all these things, he makes it look easier that it is. It will take time to practice and I don't have that time, but I use them anyway out of politeness and sadly leave my icing bag to the side. It will take a while to get used to the paddle. It is not slow and neat like my icing bag, but fast and messy. Speed wins the draw.

Grouting has to be done quickly, it sets like cement: fast, so you need to smear it on and then rub any residue off with a cloth and sponge, otherwise you will spend the lifetime of the bathroom scrapping hard grout off your tiles.

I am gradually getting a technique and so I make a large quantity of grout and smear it across the tiles, pushing it into corners and along the ridges. The bathroom is already taking shape. I need to have this finished by tomorrow morning so the plumbers can do the last fittings before they finish for Christmas and we can have the working shower we require to to move in. It would be exciting only for the weight of the missing passport hanging over us. But then my mother calls. "It's arrived."

I scream at Ronan up the stairs, "Ronan the passport has arrived, let's go."

It's all hands on deck to find a way to get it to Izzy by tomorrow evening for her early morning flight on Friday.

I abandon my grouting halfway through and dash back to our rental to get on our computers and phones. DHL offers 24-hour delivery. Great.

"No, sorry we can't guarantee that, it will be two or three days because of Brexit, because of Covid, because of Christmas, because of..."

"Is there any way?" I plead.

"Well there is our Express same day service..."

"Great, we'll go with that."

"It will be €1100 to €1200."

"WHAT?"

"Well, we send someone on the next available flight and they carry it as their hand luggage."

"What, like on their way to Bali for the luxury holiday we are paying for? No thanks."

I've lost hope again.

Ronan gets on to UPS.

"Yes, we can guarantee delivery by 2pm tomorrow. Pick up will be between 12.30 and 5pm today and it will be €33.87."

Yes, please! We book it and I'm feeling more hopeful again. Next issue is the mandatory COVID test Italy requires for anyone to enter.

Every COVID testing place in London is booked up as Boris announced at the weekend that anyone arriving in Britain only has to do a short quarantine if they have a COVID test on arrival. There are test centres pulling out of the scheme due to the overwhelming demand. But Izzy discovers there is a testing place in Stansted Airport.

So the plan is to get Izzy's passport to her by 2pm tomorrow and then for her travel the three hours to Stansted, get the test and stay overnight at an airport hotel before her early morning flight back to us the following day. All good. All getting excited again.

But then 5pm arrives in Ireland and there is no courier. I call the UPS head office.

After a long time they come back and say the driver is stuck in traffic so it may be 7pm before he reaches my parent's house. We sigh with relief, but then 7.30pm arrives and my elderly parents have sore necks from watching out the window in case they miss the precious UPS van. The UPS offices are now closed. There is no one to call.

By 9.30pm I tell my parents to go to bed. It won't be collected at this point, but my dad says he'll sit up to 11pm and watch the football just in case. The collection wasn't made.

The following morning, I sit waiting for the UPS offices to open so I can call them.

A Rosie Life In Italy 2

I get through to UPS at 9am. He is in disbelief the package was not collected. He said the depot will call me in an hour with an explanation and a new pickup time. An hour and a half passes. I call them again. They reassure me it will definitely be picked up today. They are just waiting on the driver to confirm a time. At 12.30 I call again.

This guy is not so nice, "you don't have a label?"

I'm somehow ridiculous for not having a label to read a code from and for calling again. He can see on the screen that the package is scheduled to be collected. "Yes, Madam, it will be collected today and get there by tomorrow."

Mam rings me two hours later. It has been picked up!... But the guy didn't seem to know anything about taking payment of €33 cash, as we were instructed by UPS to do. Cash to driver. No worries. I am sure UPS knows what they are doing.

Half an hour later, Mam calls again. The driver is back to return the package. It needs a label with a barcode. He can't take it without a barcode. He wants to leave the package back with them and leave. What? No!

Mam is in a fluster. She is nothing short of grabbing the guy through the window and holding him by the scruff of the neck. She hands her phone out to him. We're on video call, but he has me to his ear. "My boss says I can't take this, it doesn't have a label."

"We booked it by phone. How do I get a label?"

"I don't know, I'm only in this job three weeks," he laughs and then takes the phone down to his face, realising I am on speaker and video.

"WHAT THE HELL?" I am screaming down the phone at him, "Wear a mask! Where is your mask?"

My mam isn't wearing a mask either, I realise. She's flustered and forgot.

"Where are your masks?"

My 80+ year old parents have been in isolation away from family for nine months and this asshole has just jeopardised all this effort and hardship. He pulls up his mask from under his chin,

"Oh yeah, I forgot." He is laughing again. He reluctantly gives me his boss's number. He has to go and do deliveries. Ronan, in the meantime, is on the phone to UPS head office and they are telling us we need to reorder another collection and are basically wiping their hands of the whole situation. Their rep never issued a label. We need a label.

Now you tell us? We are both fuming.

My mam is feeling sorry for the poor lad who is as thick as a plank and thinks this whole situation is laughable.

"Leave the package and go. We'll find a different way." I want his stupid, laughing, unmasked face away from there and for my mam to disinfect her phone.

I'm looking up flights for me to go to Ireland tomorrow to get the passport and fly to London–because everything is possible, but I have forgotten COVID for a moment which makes everything not so possible.

So I ring DHL again. They can collect tomorrow and get it to London on Monday. Okay, we'll go with that. We'll need to

A Rosie Life In Italy 2

print a label and stick it on. This is the step the UPS rep skipped. My niece, who lives near my parents, will print the label and get the package ready.

There is no way they will get it from Ireland to London by this afternoon now, so there is no way she will be on the flight. The third flight missed over the passport. I don't want to move in to the house without her.

Before I tell Izzy, I Google flights on the off chance we can find something. I find one to Perugia for €33 next Wednesday the 23rd of December. Everything is costing €33. I call Izzy.

"Look, you are not going to make that flight on Friday, but I have found one for next Wednesday. We'll definitely get the passport to you by then."

Izzy books the flight.

So we wait and we can sleep because we know that God, Allah, Mother Nature and our ancestors have all been politely asked and are all working together as one to sort out what is best for our little family. What will be, will be.

Sometimes big dreams need to be adjusted. The problem now is I am running out of teabags and Izzy has packed a new supply. I need her to arrive soon more than ever.

38

CYLINDER OF GAS €37

I don't sleep much and leave early to go up to the house. The grout has solidified. The blue tiles are smeared with a white haze and the gaps between the tiles, which should be slightly concave, are like tectonic plates pushing together and new mini mountain ridges forming all over our bathroom walls. It was Izzy or the grout. Every tile now tells a story of one of my most difficult times during the pandemic. The bumpy, imperfect grout will always remind me of this moment in our family history.

We need to move in before midnight on the 22nd as Italy then goes into strict lockdown and we won't be able to get to the house after that. Our plan is to have everything moved into the house on Tuesday. The building crew have been told to be finished and out by noon on the 23rd. We will then pack up the cats, hand the keys back to Giovanni and then Ronan will go to collect Izzy at Perugia airport 30 minutes away.

Karen and John's son, Charlie, is also arriving back from boarding school the day before Izzy. He's flying into Pisa. As

A Rosie Life In Italy 2

numbers are rising in the UK, there are mutterings online about lockdowns and flights being cancelled. Karen and I phone each other throughout the day to keep each other's spirits up as much as possible.

It's an 'open' day between lockdowns, so Ronan and I go grocery shopping and pack our new kitchen full of goodies and food for Christmas week. The gas company still has not connected us to the main gas line, so Super Mario has changed the fittings on our gas pipes and we can use 'bombole' – cylinders of gas. At €37 per refill, we need to be very sparing with using the bombola for heating the radiators, as they will only last a couple of hours.

Ronan takes advantage of the freedom to move and goes to buy a dehumidifier. He comes back with two more gas heaters that were on special offer. We now have a collection of four of these ugly, bulky heaters.

"They were on special offer at the Chinese Shop," he exclaimed back at my protests of wasting money.

He's has trouble with the regulators on two of them, so now he is sitting amongst all four of them, swapping parts. They look like a troop of Daleks closing in on him, about to attack. He wins the battle. We end up with one working and three brand new non-working gas heaters which Ronan has attacked so we can't return.

Within hours of being plugged in, the dehumidifier's water box is full. We find this exciting and give each other regular reports on how high the water level gets as we move it from room to room over the following days. We're nothing short of having charts on the wall. Thankfully, the water level in the room we finally decided to use as our temporary bedroom is quite low and, with the help of one of the many heaters that Ronan felt we needed, the room warms up.

It will take a few days for the pillows, duvet and all our clothes to stop feeling damp, but we now have a cosy kitchen, sitting room, and bathroom.

On Sunday, the temperatures drop to zero overnight. Sleet hammers down, driven by strong cold winds, and the night temperatures for the next ten days are not showing any improvement. The hallway has been bloody cold but tolerable, but now it feels like a main street in northern Siberia because our beautiful double, antique, north-facing front door hangs on old hinges that leave plenty of room for daylight to enter around the edges. Over decades, a nice gap has formed on the worn step under the door where a herd of small creatures could come through, no problem, all at the same time.

I root out a heavy damask curtain I threw into the camper van last minute when we were moving from Ireland three years ago – at the time I couldn't imagine why I would need it in sunny Italy but felt it might come in handy someday.

It has been packed away under the stairs at Giovanni's for the past three years beside five jam-packed plastic storage boxes. I forget what is in these boxes, but it must be important as they have travelled with me from house to house for ten years, unopened.

They were on my list to sort through during summer lockdown but I never got around to it. They were moved from our rental to the house along with the heavy curtain bag just last week, because they are important... for some reason. Someday I will get around to opening them, but I'm so glad the heavy lined curtain has found its day of importance. We hammer up some nails and hang it.

"That should do it."

But no. The gale force 'breeze' blowing in around the door makes the heavy curtain flap around like a hanky in a hurricane.

We have changed the plan from 'making the hallway look nice for Izzy's arrival' to 'let's seal up the front door so we don't freeze to death in the coming weeks'. The Pinterest-perfect idea of holly and ivy garlands draped around the door with silver baubles is replaced with Styrofoam stuck into gaps which is promptly spat out by the force of the northern 'breeze'. As we develop a technique of one holding the Styrofoam in place while the other duct tapes it down, I mutter my old favourite line, "Under the Tuscan Sun, my ass."

Bubble wrap I've kept from all the online deliveries I've had in the last few weeks and leftover insulation from the roof all play a role in our Star Ship recreation efforts. The heavy curtain is rehung and flaps less.

"At least the silver duct-tape is staying within a Christmas colour theme and, if you squint your eyes, the broken off pieces from the Styrofoam swirling in the mini cyclones in the corners give a snowglobe effect."

Luca stops sweeping up the last of the rubble in the hall. "Squint to the point of closing? You have such a good imagination, Mam."

Opening the front door again won't happen until the spring, so the decoration of the hallway will wait. We'll just hibernate until this cold spell is over. The hallway is still cold, but we feel less likely to meet a family of penguins that got in under the gap of the door when we cross it now.

We are still doing mad dashes back and forth with van loads and carloads of stuff. Moving always seems to be a slow process for us. One house move took two years. This one feels as long.

Considering we only brought over a camper van of stuff from Ireland three years ago, including a bin bag of kitchen garbage instead of a bag of much-loved clothes, we seem to have gathered an endless amount of 'stuff' that just keeps seeping from every orifice of the house every time we think we are near finished.

The timing of our move, during the peak of the pandemic, means that friends who would have normally come to help us couldn't get here, so it is just us. And with Luca under pressure to get his college assessment stuff finished, it ruled him out a lot of the days. Ronan managed to deconstruct the large, fitted wardrobe and fit it in the van with only one heated session of me shouting at him about how he 'should' do it from the bedroom doorway.

A few days ago he got up earlier than usual and went up to collect the three kitchen units for the guest kitchen from the storage shed and came back and unloaded six units and an oven before I could point out

"That's not our kitchen... when did we buy an oven?"

"I don't know. I just took what was there."

A Rosie Life In Italy 2

"Ronan, that's Giovanni's new kitchen that he's installing after we leave."

So Ronan packed the six heavy units and oven back into the van for a second time and unloaded it a third time and then loaded our correct guest kitchen, and brought it back. It's things like this that add to the length of our moving experiences.

The last thing to be moved was our olive garden bench that Ronan carved from a fallen olive tree Lucia gave us from her olive grove.

"Take the bloody thing, I have 4000 more," were her gifting words.

Olive wood is dense and heavy, but I love the bench and I didn't want it left behind. Fair play to Ronan and a few more 'encouraging' directions from me, we got it into the van. With the last push Ronan's back finally gave in.

It happens now and then and was bound to happen with all the heavy lifting, which he isn't supposed to be doing. The timing of the last push of the last thing was perfect.

I insist he have a few days' rest with painkillers so he can stop looking like a neanderthal before Izzy arrives and can be back standing upright. Our stuff is piled in rooms, mingling and losing itself amongst the stuff the previous inhabitants left behind in the house.

Ronan may be a neanderthal, but at least we have everything in except Luca's fold-out bed and computer, the TV, the cats and Luca himself. And the bathroom will be useable in 24 hours as the plumbers are installing the sink and shower fittings. We are all set. All we need to do is wait for Izzy to arrive.

Lying in bed that night, I check the news. Boris Johnson has had an emergency press conference. The fast-moving new variant of the virus, which he says is thought to be 70% more transmissible than existing strains, appears to be driving a rapid spread of new infections in London. This is not good. This is not good at all.

39

NEW MR HAPPY MUG: €13.99

The following morning, the handle broke off my Mr Happy Mug mid-slurp. On it's descent to the floor I caught it and saved his face but the handle sliced my thumb a little on the way. Yes, Mr Happy bit me.

I still remain somewhat hopeful, as the courier is on his way. He'll be there today. It's the 21st of December, the shortest day of the year, but it feels the longest.

"They might stop flights." Karen has been up all night following the breaking news updates from London of the new variant. "There are strong rumours online that Italy is going to close it's borders."

With her words, my shoulders have turned to rocks. They can't get any closer to my ears. I've taken up biting my nails, made brittle from tile cement and grout.

"They can't, not before Christmas."

But they can.

By late afternoon Karen texts, "They've closed the borders with the UK. Charlie's plane has been stopped on the runway for the last hour. It was the last one to take off. Charlie texted just before they took off to say the pilot said he was going to take a chance but they might be turned back in Pisa."

"I can't believe this is happening, Ronan. She's not going to get here."

I call Izzy. "It's bad news, love. Italy has closed the border. I don't think you will be able to get here."

Before she can answer, her doorbell rings and she brings the phone to the door. I watch as the courier hands her the long-awaited package.

"Look what just arrived." The irony amuses us rather than tipping us into complete despair.

"It's only one day Mam, I'll get to you the week after. This has all just been ridiculous. I'll just forget it's Christmas, we'll celebrate in January or whenever. Dave and my friends will be back in London the day after Christmas. Don't worry."

There's nothing either of us can say.

"How about flying to Ireland and spending it with family there?" I suggest.

"All the flights to Ireland have been cancelled too. I saw it on the internet."

She has just given up. Resigned herself to being on her own in dreary London during the time of year we treasure most. We are both forcing ourselves to belittle it to 'just another day'.

"Let's have a think about it. Let me check a few things and get back to you."

I need time to think. I can't have my little girl sitting by herself on Christmas Day. I also need to see what the press announcements are saying in the background. I'm worried about Charlie. The two and a half hours of his flight slowly ticks by. But then Karen texts; "He has landed. They weren't going to let them through, but they have now. John has him in the car."

In London, things go from bad to worse. It's now evening. The most severe tier of lockdown is announced for parts of London and a stay-at-home order has been issued. It includes the area where Izzy is. People elsewhere will not be allowed to travel into a tier-four area. The restrictions will last for two weeks, with the first review due on 30th of December. Johnson acknowledged it is "unquestionably a difficult moment" in the Coronavirus crisis but insists that things would be "radically different" by Easter due to the vaccine. There seems no way out of London. She has nowhere to run.

"Mam, they are saying this could last until Easter." Izzy is looking desperate. "Dave just called. There is a bus to Scotland leaving at midnight. In two hours. What will I do?"

"How long will it take a taxi to get you to the bus station?"

"An hour and a half, maybe a little longer if there's traffic."

I feel like I am trying to get her out of Eastern Europe before the wall came down.

"Grab what you can and get on that bus. Get Dave to buy you a ticket while you make your way there, don't stop, just go and get to the bus station immediately. Go."

"What if I'm stopped?"

"Just look like you are going home from work, don't bring a suitcase. Don't pack, just take your hand luggage bag you had for the plane. Keep your head down and just keep going."

So many times during these past nine months, things have been put into perspective, and this is one of those times. I am no longer thinking of my own happiness, or dwelling on how sad I will be without her here. I am no longer thinking of the perfect Christmas vision. I am only thinking of her happiness, of her not being lonely.

She flees, and we hold our breath.

40

LOCKSMITH: €500

While Izzy is on her way to the station, a ban on travelling to the rest of the UK is announced.

"Just keep going," both me and Ronan text several times. The music from The Great Escape is running through my head on repeat.

She keeps us posted with a blow-by-blow account; "There are police in the station but they are not stopping anyone... I'm on the bus... It's eerie."

We hold our breath. She's made it to the bus, but will it be allowed to leave the station?

Eventually she texts; "We're moving. It's going!"

An hour later, I see a news bulletin that Scotland is closing its borders to England. Is she going to be turned back? I hardly sleep a wink all night as we wait for the morning light and her 9am arrival time.

I am semi-delirious from tension and lack of sleep. I start thinking of the situation as a blurb for something cheesy on Netflix.

'Girl is on her way from London to Italy to be with her family for Christmas but loses passport. Her new passport gets lost in the mail. Time is running out – her friends have all left for Christmas and soon she won't have anywhere to live.

Then disaster hits. Zombies invade London, the city goes into emergency lockdown, and no one is permitted to leave. As soon as her new passport is delivered, Italy closes its border with the UK. Where will she go? What will she do? Will it be a slice of turkey alone for Christmas? It's all looking very dismal. In the meantime, her mother realises she can tile a bathroom much quicker when very stressed. There is always a positive.'

We wouldn't even watch it on Netflix as we would say it is far too corny, and the ending sounds predictable. There is no way her mother will get the bathroom finished. But this is real life and 2020 when nothing is predictable anymore.

Eventually at 9.10am we get the text we've been waiting for. "I'm here! The bus has stopped and I can see Dave waiting for me."

As Dave's family work in the emergency services, they are both in agreement to stay at a distance from each other until Izzy has a negative COVID test. It will take two days and, until that happens, she will stay in isolation in the house. But she is there. It's such a relief that she will spend Christmas with a family rather than by herself.

A Rosie Life In Italy 2

Christmas means families being together. There are so many torn apart this year, we are not the only ones. Although I do feel deprived of a whole precious month of our time together, the last 24 hours put everything into perspective. She is healthy; we are healthy.

Christmas this year is going to be different and memorable for different reasons.

For instance, Ronan is walking around like a neanderthal.

"Izzy will get here somehow after Christmas, so we will see her in the next couple of weeks. Let's just make the most of it. We'll celebrate Christmas properly together when she gets here."

Luca and Ronan agree.

"Will we be able to cook Christmas dinner in the new kitchen?" asks Luca skeptically as the Christmas dinner the previous two Christmases were a bit of a struggle at the rental.

"Bloody right, we are cooking dinner in that gorgeous kitchen! And we will be using all the surfaces. But we are missing one thing... a Christmas tree. Let's go find the biggest one we can."

Luca and Ronan know my obsession with big fat Christmas trees. Every year we go shopping for it together as a family and Izzy and I would spend a day decorating the tree and the house. This year would be different in so many ways.

Finding a gigantic Christmas tree in Italy is difficult, I discover. The shops just have little ones. Of course, it's a Mediterranean country so they do not have Christmas tree woods and most people live in apartments around where we are, so there is probably no demand for big trees. None of the trees will do. I need a big tree. Eventually I find a big, growing tree in a pot in a garden centre. It's quite lopsided but will do perfectly, as it will still be alive when Izzy gets here. There is no way it will fit in the car, so we arrange to come the following day in the van to collect it.

The locksmith arrives and puts new front and back door locks on and new sliding bolts on the two ground floor French doors. A surprising €500 later, our house is secure, and we are handed keys to the front door for the first time. I make two copies of them and wrap them for under the tree, one set for Luca and one for Izzy.

Danny Boy finishes installing the hand-basin and the kitchen sink and wishes us luck and a happy Christmas before pulling out of the drive for the final time in what was the strangest year in all our lives.

"We need a sofa," Ronan is standing in the empty but prepped sitting room, thinking aloud. Within minutes he is lugging the dust-filled diarrhoea corduroy three-seater out from the front room where all the left furniture is stacked.

"Oh no, not that." I'm looking in horror at the cheap retro sofa that somehow has avoided the 'definitely to be dumped pile'. It looks like it is breathing and puffing out dragon breath dust clouds.

"Give it a chance." Ronan bypasses the sitting room and drags it out through the French doors into the garden, where he whacks the hell out of it until all the clouds of dust lessen before he pulls it back in and plonks down on it. I reluctantly check under the seat cushions. There is still plastic on the underside frame, so it must have been fairly new before they closed up the house. The back and cushions are foam, and there is no sign of spiders, scorpions, or any nests being built. It's actually in perfect shape other than the dust.

I cautiously sit beside Ronan, and with his arm around me, the sofa is surprisingly comfortable. It's a good size and fits perfectly.

"Well, with a few throws and cushions it will do the job until we find the one we want."

Luca helps Ronan carry out a gold glass square coffee table with tubular aluminium legs and castors which was also in the 'definitely to be dumped' pile.

"I've seen these before in other people's houses," says Luca in all seriousness. At 17, he cannot remember living in a house with a proper sitting room setup with a three-piece suite and a coffee table. We had one until he was three, but have been in unfinished renovation projects and small rentals since then. This home will be different. It will be finished and it will be beautiful.

Now that we have locks, we can lock up the house and stay in our rental for the last time. We have put it back to the way we got it, with Giovanni's mattresses and furniture in place, so we have beds to sleep on. Luca has done a good job of cleaning the house from top to bottom while we have been working on the other house, but as always we find there are still things lying around that need to be moved and corners still to be cleared and cleaned.

But after a couple of frantic hours we have the big TV, bedding, Luca's computer and baskets of laundry and potted plants off the terrace, in the back of the van.

I have my last cup of tea from my flask on the terrace overlooking the silvery lake. In the distance to the left, the ancient town of Passignano is lit with the amber light of the winter sun. Amber light signals you can move now, but take it easy.

One last walk around the back field with Asha. It was this field walk that got us through lockdown and where I learned about the different flora and fauna of this country that I hope I will feel at home in soon. Barney, the wild boar baby Asha tried to befriend, the birds, the caterpillars, the butterflies, the chickpeas, the wildflowers, the deer tracks. The changing light of the changing seasons. The place I came to have a moment to myself, to regroup.

"Come on," shouts Ronan from the back of the house, snapping me out of my sentimental thoughts. "We have the Christmas tree to collect before the shop closes."

I do an effort of a jog back up the garden, with Asha doing a pretend run beside me to make me feel less incapable. She immediately jumps into the van and takes her place. The same way she did three years previously when we packed up the same van and headed for Rosslare Ferry Port and left Ireland bound for Italy. She's ready to be our guardian on our next adventure.

I look down and still have a mug in my hand. "Oh Crap, we don't have a kettle at the new house. How did we forget to buy such an essential item when I drink twenty cups of tea per day?"

"We'll stop off at the electric shop on the way. It's near the garden centre. But we have to hurry. They will all be closing for the Christmas break in an hour."

So we wave goodbye to the farm and chug out of Giovanni's farm gates for the last time.

41

CHRISTMAS TREE: €125

The first stop is the electric shop. Mask on, I run into the shop. It doesn't take long, as there is only one type of electric kettle available. There are about fifty brands and colours of coffee machines and pasta makers, but only one kettle and it's blue. It will do. I pay and run out with the kettle in my hand. No need to waste a bag on it, it will join the menagerie of stuff in the back of the van. I still feel like I'm going to rob a place when donning a mask and doing a quick nip in to a shop.

"Go, go, go!" I shout at Ronan as I jump into the front of the van beside Luca. It still reminds me of the grocery shopping trips we had during early lockdowns.

Next stop the garden centre. Ronan is less neanderthal-ish, but it takes both Ronan and Luca's strength to carry out the weighty tree in its large bucket filled with clay. We gather an audience of last-minute shoppers being pushed out as the shop closes up.

A Rosie Life In Italy 2

They look on at our Irish 20-year-old van stuffed with the oddest assortment of items jammed against the windows including near-dead potted plants, carriers with two meowing cats, duvets, mismatched shoes, a TV, a kettle, a yelping small dog and a giant German shepherd who is looking very perplexed at having to share her space with a large tree. All we need now is a partridge and a few pears.

I'm doing the "go, go, go," thing again as we pull slowly out onto the road.

Working all hours to get the house into a semi-fit state to move into, pandemic restrictions and all the passport and travel drama of the last few weeks hasn't given me or Ronan any time to give much thought to Christmas presents. I had ordered stuff and got it online for Luca and Izzy, but we had both forgotten about each other. Also, being close to divorcing each other over tiling, grouting, painting and repair techniques has not induced any romantic feelings.

"Ronan, I'm sorry, but I haven't had time to get you a gift."

It's the only thing making me feel a little sad because I love having things wrapped under the tree and gift-giving at Christmas. Even if it is a crap gift, it resurrects the excited anticipation I had as a child as the mountain of gifts grew in the weeks up to Christmas, with eight of us in the house and about thirty aunts and uncles visiting.

"I haven't got you one either... but we'll soon fix that." He swings the van into the car park of the last shop still open.

"Twenty euro max spend each, okay?" he smiles.

"The Chinese shop?" It's not exactly Tiffany's, but it will do.

We needed to be quick. It is getting dark, and they are getting ready to close. I pick up a box with a man's face on it in the cosmetics aisle near the cash till. I didn't have my glasses on, but you can't go wrong with a man-gadget for Ronan.

Walking back to the van, he tells me he's bought me lingerie.

"From the Chinese shop? This should be interesting."

It's dark by the time we pull into the driveway of the place we are going to live in for possibly the rest of our lives. I can't call it home yet. That will take time. It will take us getting to know its creaks and corners, for our feelings and smells to mingle with its structure, for us all to find our favourite places and the things that irritate us. The things we love and the things we want to change. And for Izzy to arrive. Then it will be home. For now, there's a bed frame in the kitchen, rubble in the bedrooms, a bathroom without a door, but we're in.

Everything is still in boxes, clothes and bed linens in black plastic bags so as not to get damp, but all our 'stuff' is here now and we can fully focus on making this place our own.

Ronan lights up the stove before he and Luca drag the tree in. I already have the new kettle on and have thrown two blue cotton throws I got in the Chinese Shop over the corduroy sofa and empty the sack of cushions onto it. It looks better already. The cats are playing chasing up and down the stairs, and the dogs are looking on amused. Walking back into the sitting room, I notice a small, folded card on the floor near the hearth.

"What's that?" Ronan asks as I lift it up.

"It's a Christmas gift card. Like the ones we used to stick on a present to say who it's for when we were kids."

There's an old-fashioned flower print on the front and inside on the white card that has yellowed in the corners with age 'Buon Natale' is printed.

"Who's it from?" Ronan is eagerly opening the box of the new TV.

"I think... the house?" I can't think of any other explanation of where it came from.

He takes it from my hand and looks at it momentarily. "Heh... that's weird... She must have woken from her surgery, and she's happy enough with the result to send Christmas cards then?"

I place it delicately on the mantle beside the Christmas card from my mam, lingering a moment to try to find a logical explanation of how it came to be on the floor, but failing.

We've had a long day of packing and some unpacking. While looking for the Christmas decorations box with Luca's help, we pulled out a box of books from Paolo's shelves we still haven't gone through. The binding of a thin, leather-bound one attracts my eye. I pull it out and it's better than I expected.

"It's a photo album!"

Inside are the monochrome faces of those who lived, loved and laughed before us in the rooms of the Workhouse. There are studio portraits of Paolo as a cute, curly-headed toddler, him when he was in his early 20s, a faded photo of him in an African jungle and the last one at the back is a dapper older man wearing a white fedora, smart suit pants and pressed short-sleeved shirt, camera hanging from a strap around his neck. He is looking towards the camera, smiling at us.

In the same box under the photo album, there's an accordion music book and booklets of songs with Paolo's signature on them.

"He must have played and sang too. Can you imagine this house in the 20's, 30's, 40's and 50s – the parties they must have had with Miranda dishing out the champagne in her saucer glasses and Paolo playing the accordion and singing his heart out?"

"With his learning to speak English like a gentleman record on the gramophone," grins Luca. He has grown as fond as I have for the old guy we have never met.

By the time I have got down the stairs and into the warm sitting room with the box of decorations, Luca has put on a Christmas playlist of Italian accordion music. I threw the decorations on the tree. It's not being done with the same care and attention I normally do with Izzy. But it will do. Christmas is different this year.

"I know we normally open presents on Christmas eve," says Ronan, "but I think you would appreciate what I got you now."

Ronan and I scramble to find the gifts we had bought each other amongst the moving boxes and bags, wrap them 'carefully' in the shopping bags they came in, and hand them to each other. The gadget I got Ronan turns out to be nasal hair trimmer, and he hadn't read the slogan on the 'sexy' lingerie he'd bought me. It is not sexy lingerie but synthetic fluffy PJs, with 'Frenemies' spelt incorrectly splashed across the front.

"Put them on. They look cosy."

I'm not pushed, but I don't want to insult the gift he spent so much of five minutes to buy, and anyway there is something I have been dying to do. I go into my finished tiled bathroom and turn on the beautiful brass rain shower. Within seconds, warm water is raining on me, easing my aching bones, rewarding me for all the work I have done to build its surroundings and comforting me. It's too good to get out of, but I reluctantly do, having lost track of time. The Frenemies PJs are fantastically comfy.

By the time I come out, the pets have found their favourite spot in front of the pellet stove; the lads are putting together the new TV stand – I'll soon be called on to read the instructions and it will all be grand. There's a turkey breast in the fridge for roasting on Christmas day and I'm having a glass of Baileys.

"What's this?" I point at a gift under the tree that I didn't put there.

"It's the present I got you Mam. Open it."

I don't need encouragement. I rip the paper open. "It's a book to record our family history. I've seen how you are loving discovering the history of this place, so I thought you'd like it."

"Like it, I love it!" Flicking through the pages if falls open on grand uncles and aunts.

"You can add your uncle that we went to see in France."

It took me a few seconds to realise who he was talking about. "Oh, you mean James Carroll, who the beautiful French woman is looking after... I think we should add Paolo as an adopted Italian uncle."

"Can we do that?"

"Why not? None of his blood relatives were interested in his stuff, but he's part of our history now."

Izzy calls excited. "My Covid test came back negative and David's family are lovely!"

She is out of her isolation room and is already enjoying making Christmas cookies with her boyfriend's sister. She sends a picture of herself kissing David underneath the mistletoe with the backdrop of a warm, cosy room, Christmas lights twinkling and an open fire blazing.

As I sip my Baileys beside the sparkling Christmas tree lights and wait for the lads to call on me to read the TV stand assembly instructions, my imagination creates the blurb of the next Netflix instalment to the one I came up with a few days ago;

"Handsome love interest calls from Scotland; There's a bus at midnight. Get on it. Come live with my family until you can get to yours. She flees, gets the bus with a bag of grapes, losing a slipper on the way. Scotland has closed its borders to the Zombies, but she makes it through just in time to kiss the guy under the mistletoe and have a wonderful Christmas with his family."

Yep, it would be way too corny to watch, but I'm relieved that she'll spend Christmas with a fun and loving family in a safe 'bubble'. She will get to us when it is safe to do so.

She made it. We made it. The house is no longer the Workhouse, it's becoming a home and will need a new name. Who knows what the next year holds for us all and the house. It can't be as challenging as this year, can it?

If you enjoyed my story please do post a review on Amazon, it means a lot!

Sign up for house and book updates on www.rosiemeleady.com

A Rosie Life In Italy Book 3: Should I Stay or Should I Go is available for pre-order through Amazon.

ACKNOWLEDGMENTS

Many thanks to:

Marco Moretti for designing another great front cover.

Suzy Pope for her editing skills.

My FB group (@arosielifeinitaly) who constantly encourage our house reno 'efforts' and cheer our successes.

My beta readers for taking the time to read through my errors!

ABOUT THE AUTHOR

Dubliner Rosie Meleady has been a magazine publisher and editor since 1994. She won the International Women in Publishing Award 1996 at the ripe old age of 24. She couldn't attend the award ceremony in London as she decided it would also be a good day to give birth.

She now lives happily ever after in Italy disguised as a wedding planner, while renovating the villa and writing long into the night.

Follow Rosie on her blog and social media: www.rosiemeleady.com

Printed in Great Britain
by Amazon